The Hate Handbook

The Hate Handbook

Oppressors, Victims, and Fighters

Martin Oppenheimer

LEXINGTON BOOKS

A Division of
ROWMAN & LITTLEFIELD PUBLISHERS, INC.
Lanham • Boulder • New York • Toronto • Oxford

LEXINGTON BOOKS

A division of Rowman & Littlefield Publishers, Inc.
A wholly owned subsidary of The Rowman & Littlefield Publishing Group, Inc.
4501 Forbes Boulevard, Suite 200
Lanham, MD 20706

PO Box 317
Oxford
OX2 9RU, UK

British Library Cataloguing in Publication Information Available

Library of Congress Cataloging-in-Publication Data

Oppenheimer, Martin.
    The hate handbook : oppressors, victims, and fighters / Martin Oppenheimer.
        p. cm.
    Includes bibliographical references and index.
    ISBN 0-7391-1054-3 (hardcover : alk. paper)—ISBN 0-7391-1055-1 (pbk. : alk.
paper)
    1. Social conflict. 2. Hate. 3. Equality. 4. Oppression (Psychology) 5. Violence.
6. Group identity. 7. Social change. I. Title.

HM1121.O67 2005
302.5'4—dc22   2005016732

Printed in the United States of America

∞™ The paper used in this publication meets the minimum requirements of
American National Standard for Information Sciences—Permanence of Paper
for Printed Library Materials, ANSI/NISO Z39.48-1992.

For Ari and Jai
May they see the birth of a better world

Contents

Prologue: Is This Trip Really Necessary?

$\mathcal{I}$f you go to any online book seller, or to any respectable library, you will find listings for a dozen or more books on hate, bigotry, prejudice, and the like, not to mention books on racism, anti-Semitism, mass murder, and atrocities of many kinds in many places and historical times (some of them included in the bibliography). Why another one?

People write books, create art, play musical instruments, not because we don't have enough books, or artists, or musicians, but because they have to. It is their mission, their reason for being. I had to write this book to try to answer, for myself (and hopefully for others) the perennial question: Why do people hate? How can human beings do the horrifying things they do to other human beings? Many have peered into this abyss; many have concluded that there ultimately is no full answer, and have become pessimists about the human condition. Yet there is another side to the question: How do people manage, despite the obstacles, to resist those who hate and oppress them? What do they do to fight back? I wanted in some systematic way to try to answer that question as well. That is the purpose of this book.

How did it all begin? My first direct personal exposure to racial bigotry was back in 1943 when I was a 13-year-old going to school in South Jersey, which is, as you may or may not know, below the Mason-Dixon line. Not so many years earlier (and indeed once in a while even nowadays) the Ku Klux Klan was active in the area. We farm kids rode a school bus, and one day two little black kids, I think the children of a farm laborer family, got on, and the other kids started in on them with some racist insults, and I, the only Jew on the bus, stood up in the aisle and said something like "why don't you leave them alone, they haven't done anything to you." That was the moment I graduated from being just a Christ-killer (being harassed every Easter) to also being a "nigger-lover." Remember this was in the middle of the war against fascism. I was not yet old enough to find this a bit ironic.

Why did I stand up for those children? Later on I learned what this was called: identifying with the oppressed. There is a certain tendency among Jews to do this: two of the three volunteers who were murdered by the Ku Klux Klan in Mississippi during Freedom Summer's voter registration campaign in 1964 were Jewish. But there was more to my action than that. I was not just any farm kid. My parents and I were refugees from Hitler's Germany. They had had direct exposure to a kind of racial bigotry called anti-Semitism, and I surely was aware of that.

This was about the same time I read Richard Wright's *Black Boy*, which had been published in 1937, the year I arrived in this country to escape Nazism. That book was my introduction to "racial etiquette" in the South, a place that seemed pretty far away from New Jersey, even South Jersey, at the time.

Some years later, having read many more books by then, I was drafted into the Army in what was called the U.N. Police Action in Korea, a war in which more than 50,000 U.S. soldiers died to protect the South Korean dictatorship from what we were told by some politicians were the Slavo-Mongolian hordes. I was flown to Fort McClellan, Alabama, just outside Anniston, where, just down the road only a few years later (1961) the Klan would burn down the integrationist Freedom Rider bus under the watchful eyes of the FBI, another interesting example of racial etiquette. But that was still to come.

On the bus ride from Birmingham airport to Ft. McClellan we were lectured by the good ol' boy bus driver on racial etiquette when we stopped at a roadside diner for a break. He pointed to the rear of the place, showing us where the "colored boys" were to go. There was a real sense of shock among the Yankee draftees, and a lot of pretty audible expressions of disgust, and nobody got off the bus, black or white. The driver took this miniprotest as an opportunity to instruct us that we'd have to learn how things were done "down here," and to go along with the local mores, on the basis that after all as outsiders we couldn't possibly understand "our problem."

I was sitting next to a black draftee from New York City who was flabbergasted at all this. He had no inkling of what was in store for him down there off post, and it fell to me to clue him in as best as I could. The post itself of course was integrated thanks to Harry Truman's early version of affirmative action, against which not even our Southern drill sergeants raised the slightest overt protest.

Many years later, in the spring of 1995, I happened to attend the meetings of the Eastern Sociological Society, a professional organization of sociologists, and heard a talk by Chuck Willie, a well-known and highly respected black sociologist. He had once been president of the society. One thing he talked about triggered some memories: in the context of arguing in favor of multiculturalism, he said that all minorities were marginal people, and marginal people, he argued, were very useful to society in that they are able to transcend narrow group loyalties to speak to more universal truths, while also contributing immensely to the richness of the overall culture. Thin empirical ice, I thought, since being on the fringes of society was a defining characteristic of Hitler's supporters, and is as typical of today's skinheads and some ultra-right-wing militia types as it was of yesterday's Nazi brownshirts, but that aside, he did remind me of another kind of marginal people, whom I once had called "exiles at home." Willie in fact mentioned the (white Southern) sociologist Robin Williams as his prime example. Lewis Killian was another, as was Ed King, a Mississippi clergyman and sociologist who had been in the civil rights trenches since around 1960, the year of the "Negro" student sit-ins.

Back when I was doing my dissertation research, which was on the sit-ins, I would run into people like King, born and raised in the South, people we northerners called "reconstructed Southerners," the best kind there were because somewhere along the line they'd had a revelation that the way things were done just wasn't right, and that had turned them into marginal folk, internal exiles.

There were other kinds of exiles too, Yankees, at the larger universities, and singly and in pairs even at the smaller so-called Negro colleges, many of which were (and are) church-related. There were faculty members (some soon to be fired for supporting their students in the sit-ins), human relations activists working for, say, Quaker organizations, or connected to the Highlander Folk School (Myles Horton being an example), some were premature Peace Corps do-gooder types before there was a Peace Corps or Vista Volunteers, because it sure seemed there was a lot of good to be done, especially in the segregated South of those days. They all helped teach me, in my travels, about some of the byways of bigotry.

The racial etiquette of the time required that white people, most especially white women, not traffic with black people in public, period. In the armed forces, on post okay, off post no. Later, as the etiquette got broken more and more frequently by civil rights activists, Southern whites had to try to figure out how to understand it, that is, they had to try to rationalize what they saw, fit it into their mind-set, when they saw the whites picket on the line with the black students and their black community supporters. For someone who had been raised in bigotry, there was no logic that could fit the white picket, no matter that these integrationists' grandfathers might have fought with Lee. The idea that the white picket was just a good guy wanting to help the downtrodden was not acceptable. The white picket had to be reinterpreted, deconstructed, as people would say nowadays, but in a certain kind of way that would not break through or challenge the old ways of understanding things. So white pickets had to be reinterpreted as either light-skinned "Negroes," which excused them in a way, let them off a little degree, for the Negro is invisible and the Negro picket is not really getting through to the segregationist conscience, or at least not very often back then. Or they are outside troublemakers, "comm-u-nists," or, much worse, renegades, that is to say race traitors. For no white, no real Southerner, could do this thing, this walking with the sign, which was like wanting a Negro to marry their sister.

When the picket was a woman it was worse, much worse. She had to be redefined as a whore, for any woman who wanted integration wanted intercourse, and ladies surely didn't want that. Only "Negro girls" and whores. What this all meant concretely was that violence directed at demonstrators sometimes increased with the presence of whites, especially white women, and white women were particular targets, not only of men but even more so of other white women for whom the presence of the white integrationist woman symbolized not just immediate clear and present danger to their daughters, not just the collapse of family, church, and private property, but virtually the collapse of Western civilization itself.

Of course everyone knew that all this was bogus, and even kind of insane, for everyone knew the definition of a Southern gentleman in those days: one who will sleep with his Negro servant at night and refuse to sit next to her on the bus the next day. Natives of Durham always noted with pride the beautiful home built by a prominent tobacco-fortune-builder for his black mistress. Let 'em into the schools? Can't do that, they're immoral. Integrate the colleges? What's good enough for my daughter, said a prominent U.S. senator from those parts not that long ago of his black offspring, who was attending a black college, is good enough for everybody. We now know that this was Senator Strom Thurmond. The story back then was that a black chauffeur took her to and from the college every day in a limo. Fact, it was said, not fiction, and probably not limited to one senator, either. Exiles, Yankee or homegrown, had to live with that kind of insanity.

Bigotry translated into etiquette took, at least for us outsiders, us tourists, some odd turns. In Columbia, South Carolina, the capital, there is a small traditionally black Baptist college called Benedict. It was on the American Association of University Professors' list of censured institutions for firing integrationist faculty for about as many years as my alma mater, Temple University, was on the list for firing a philosopher who refused to testify before The House Un-American Activities Committee in the '50s. Anyway, in 1961 I interviewed a white teacher at Benedict, and that evening she and some of her students took me to a local black ribs place. Now, "took" was more complicated than it might seem today. Who was going to drive the car, and who was going to sit where, in order to avoid hassles? As veterans of the movement know, there were rules to all that: In 1961 the whites sat in the back of the car, the black students drove. Likewise, when it came time to take me back to the rooming house where I was staying, I sat in the back, and they dropped me off several blocks away so I, obviously a Yankee, wouldn't be asked a whole lot of possibly very hostile questions by the landlady.

All this of course was pretty small beer compared to the larger picture, and the struggles that were still to come after 1960. When I was in the army, it was not that unusual to hear some of the northern boys, in the face of Southern white culture, which seemed to them to consist mostly of inedible food (grits), weak beer, dreadful music (a guy dressed in a white suit named Faron Young was the rage at the time), and separate water fountains, regret that Sherman hadn't done a better job. But all this would change in just a few more years, after the Montgomery bus boycott and the sit-ins of 1960, the Freedom Rides, the voter registration campaigns, and in general the civil rights movement.

After that a lot of people besides Martin Luther King Jr. had a dream, especially after John Kennedy was elected. But pretty soon it became clearer and clearer that it was one thing to insure a good climate for investment in the South by integrating some public facilities, quite another to solve the more fundamental issues of the African-American community, especially in the North. How often have we heard the word *crisis?* By the mid-1960s the country had become just one big permanent crisis.

Lyndon Johnson's war on poverty pretty soon became Lyndon Johnson's war against the Vietnamese, and when—50,000 plus American and millions of Vietnamese casualties later—that was over, it became every president's war against the "lower orders," as the British say, the subaltern classes. In between somewhere, at the high and low point of all the movements of the '60s, in the glorious/disastrous year of 1968 Reverend King was assassinated. I was in Boston at the Eastern Sociological Society Meetings at the time, and in our hotel we could hear the fire sirens, and stepping outside could smell the smoke from the fires set by the enraged black citizens just a few miles from the place where the American Revolution's first shot had been fired.

Nowadays, some of my African-American students seem to feel that nothing has changed, that it was all a waste of time. Some at least seem to agree with Malcolm X, who is reported to have scoffed, "Why are they asking the white man for a cup of coffee?" (He was referring to the campaign, in 1960, to integrate lunch counters at "five-and-ten" stores such as Woolworth's, in the Southern and border states.) As we look around, however, it is clear they speak from a lack of historical awareness. First and foremost, the movement led, ultimately, to larger and larger numbers of blacks entering the political process, and holding public office. As Frances Piven and Richard Cloward said in *Poor People's Movements*, "the deepest meaning of the winning of democratic political rights is that the historical primacy of terror as a means of social control has been substantially diminished. The reduction of terror in the everyday life of a people is always in itself an important gain." To quote Aldon Morris in *The Origins of the Civil Rights Movement*, "The South is a different place today. . . . Southern blacks now live in a world . . . that does not automatically strip them of human dignity."

It would only be a small exaggeration to say that in 1953, when I was at Fort McClellan, Alabama, black people in the American South had more in common with Africans in South Africa than they had with African-Americans in, say, New York or California. Social movements have fundamentally changed all of that, fortunately in South Africa as well. That was their achievement, and to the extent that we participated, our achievement also.

There's a documentary film called *Union Maids* in which an old woman long active in the labor and radical movement is asked whether she thought it had all been worth it. "I regret nothing," she replies, "for the movement gave purpose to my life." That is what movements do, they give purpose to one's life (but unfortunately this cuts both ways: the Nazi movement also gave purpose to many people's lives).

For a long time, my commitment has been to movements that give purpose to people's lives in a positive way, toward positive social changes that enhance the human potential and liberate us from oppression and exploitation. Those movements constitute my hope. But there is the other, the fearful side. There are destructive forces, and people who do horrifying things.

This volume is going to look at hate, the kind we generally associate with the term *bigotry*. Following an introductory chapter, we will try to figure out how bigotry works (that is, how people use it to make sense out of their very insecure, confusing, and rapidly changing lives), and how people justify it despite their various religions' messages of tolerance (chapter 2). We will examine the language of oppression: the very fascinating if somewhat depressing idea that the oppression of a political and economic kind is linked to sexual oppression, and sexual language, and how jobs that are oppressive are often those held disproportionally by women, and minorities (chapter 3). In chapter 4 we will tackle the complicated issue of ethnocentrism, nationalism, and xenophobia in the wider world today, with the aim of trying to separate out the different issues faced by nations with different kinds of minority "problems." Chapter 5 deals with right-wing extremism, focusing mostly on the U.S. We'll look at different kinds of conspiracy theories, we'll try to differentiate between different forms of right-wing extremism, and we'll examine some of the prescriptions that people have come up with over the years to combat hate movements. Then in chapter 6 we will look at what many people probably see as the ultimate form of hatred's result: terrorism, an often misused and misunderstood term but a phenomenon that, if carefully defined and analyzed, gives us further insights into hatred and hopefully how to combat it.

In the final chapter, we will look at how oppressed people fight back psychologically and politically, as individuals and in social movement form. Today there are new movements, some related to the continuing struggle of the oppressed, others less obviously so, yet in the final analysis also connected to the quest for the kinds of positive social change that affect all oppressed and exploited people.

But there are also "retro" movements that seek to overturn the gains of the past half-century, movements that promise hope in the short run but are counterproductive in terms of expanding human rights and opening possibilities for the development of the human potential. On the one hand, there is the vast "global justice" movement that engages hundreds of thousands throughout the world in a variety of struggles against the depredations of global capital. And there are many, many local movements on issues ranging from fighting the construction of a Wal-Mart superstore to electing public officials committed to obtaining living wages, building affordable housing, and ending hunger. On the other hand, there is the fundamentalist backlash against all manifestations of modernity, of the Enlightenment values associated with the American and French revolutions in particular. We need to understand both the positive and the reactive.

The reader won't find firm prescriptions, no absolute answers to the question of how to deal with hatred, bigotry, and the movements that utilize them, in this book. But maybe we can come up with some ideas that will help us develop positive policies and ways to support movements to solve some of our problems, alternative strategies that might exert some influence on those now moving in counterproductive directions. We need to figure out ways to move them from roads that are destructive, and away from fear, onto roads of hope.

Here is the problem, as historian Christopher Browning poses it in his book *Ordinary Men* (of which more later): " . . . we live in a world in which war and racism are ubiquitous, in which the powers of government, mobilization and legitimization are powerful and increasing, in which a sense of personal responsibility is increasingly attenuated by specialization and bureaucratization, and in which the peer group exerts tremendous pressures on moral norms. In such a world, I fear, modern governments that wish to commit mass murder will seldom fail in their efforts . . . to induce 'ordinary men' to become

. . . willing executioners.'" If Browning is to be proven wrong, as I am sure he dearly wishes, we have a lot to do.

Note to the reader: Full citations for all authors cited in the body of this work are found following the last chapter, except for newspaper or magazine articles, which are referenced in brackets immediately after the quotation.

Introduction:
Hate and the Struggle for Resources

*W*e are in the City of Brotherly Love, Philadelphia, at noon on a given Friday. On South 15th Street, opposite the Israeli consulate, a group of about fifteen middle-aged, respectably dressed individuals, mostly of the Jewish faith, is walking quietly in an elongated circle carrying signs calling for an end to the Israeli occupation of Palestinian territories. Across the street, in front of the consulate (which is not visible, since the offices are on an upper floor) some twenty high school and college-age youths, and a few older people, supporters of Israeli policy, are carrying signs that oppose "Palestinian terrorism." They are yelling very loudly across the street at the older group, calling them apologists for terrorism, urging them to join "Arafat's whorehouse," waving their arms, their fists clenched. The police prevent one of them from charging across the street to attack the anti-occupation group, which continues quietly to walk around. It seems that the younger group is so incensed that the word "hate" would not be out of place. Why are they so angry that they seem almost frighteningly out of control?

We are in a New Jersey suburb outside the offices of a Republican congressman. On the sidewalk a group of some twenty-five mostly middle-aged and older people, respectably dressed, is standing in a line facing the busy street. Some of them are members of a group called Military Families Speak Out. They are holding signs condemning the U.S. government for its Iraq policy, its lies about weapons of mass destruction, and its cutbacks for veterans hospitals, and calling for "an end to the occupation." Another occupation.

"Support our troops, bring them home now" is the theme. A pedestrian appears and proceeds, in a very loud voice, to curse this group with a barrage of four-letter words. He is extremely angry. The veins stand out on his throat.

1

His fists are raised. He is confronted by one of the demonstrators, a middle-aged woman wearing a T-shirt on which is printed "My son died in Iraq" and giving a date early in 2004. The man is undeterred and continues to yell, and curse, until the police urge him to move away. He continues to shout from some distance for a considerable time. He seems to be consumed by hatred for these people, who have done him no harm. Why is he so uncontrollably angry?

The difference between being "merely" prejudiced and bigoted, or being "merely" angry and hatred, becomes clearer when we look at what are called "hate crimes," offenses directed against an individual or a group simply because of membership in a racial, ethnic, religious, gender, or similar category. Hate crimes, Jack Levin and Jack McDevitt tell us in their book of that title, "tend to be *excessively brutal.*" Their victims end up in the hospital or morgue. They are perpetrated against random members of the victim category, not at specific individuals known to the perpetrator. As many members of minority groups know, since such attacks are random, "the mere decision to leave home automatically puts them at risk of being victimized." That's the way it used to be for any African-American in the Old South every day. Finally, hate crimes are usually perpetrated by a *group* of offenders, a small (or in the days of lynch mobs, large) mob. The individual participant is part of a group, indeed becomes anonymous in the group, which affords him or her encouragement. There is safety in numbers, as Levin and McDevitt put it. But the essence of the hate crime is its extreme violence. We are not, of course, talking about a bunch of high school kids scrawling swastikas on the side of a synagogue, which is also characterized technically as a hate crime. We are talking about felonious assault and battery, even homicide. We are not talking about pranks. We are talking about serious hate.

These crimes are a form of aggression. In psychology there is a phenomenon called the frustration-aggression thesis. It means, simply, that when people are frustrated, prevented from doing something (making a living, feeling secure, having sex), some form of aggression will be the result. However, there are many kinds of aggression. Some forms are internal: people aggress against themselves in the form of drug abuse, or at the extreme, suicide. Other forms are external, toward others: spouse, kids, the dog, assault, rape, most everyday homicide. Still other forms take political form, and can be positive in nature: the organization of movements to attack the sources of the oppression that has led to frustration. (We will discuss this further in chapter 7.) Hate, when it takes aggressive form, is therefore only one sort of aggressive behavior. Unfortunately, when it takes the form of large-scale social and political movements that translate into government policy, it can be genocidal in its results.

What is hate, and why do people hate? The dictionary talks about "extreme dislike." The terms *animus,* antipathy (from the Greek *anti*—against, and *patheia*—to feel, or suffer, as in the word *pathology*) occur to us. But this is not very helpful. Gordon W. Allport, whose classic *The Nature of Prejudice*, first published in 1954, distinguishes between anger, which is felt toward individuals, and is often short-lived, and hatred, which is felt against whole groups or classes of people and is directed randomly rather than against a specific individual. Hatred is more stubborn. "(T)he hater is sure that the fault lies in the object of his hate. So long as he believes this he will not feel guilty for his uncharitable state of mind." But most of the time hatred is directed at an "outgroup," the "other," usually a minority. Yet in both of the cases described here the victims are of the same ethnicity, even of similar social class. They are all, or mostly, Jews. They are all, or mostly, Christians. Yet in both cases, the perpetrators lack any sense of empathy toward their victims; it is as if those who are being attacked (only verbally, fortunately) are of a different species. How is this possible?

More broadly, why is it that in this supposedly rational early twenty-first century large groups of people hate other groups of people and murder them wholesale? Pick up the paper any day of the week: Chechnya, Bosnia, Rwanda, Myanmar, Corsica, Cyprus, the Kurds, the Basques, the IRA. Neo-Nazis, skinheads, militias, Aryan Nations, the Ku Klux Klan, Al Qaida. Jean-Marie Le Pen, David Duke, Bo Gritz, Osama bin Laden, or any one of a dozen rap music groups. The language of some of our political leaders borders on hatred as well, hatred for those who presumably hate us, for those whose allegiance is to another religious system or even to a civilization that is said to be antagonistic to ours.

There are many scientists, journalists, and, almost needless to say, politicians, who still think it has something to do with the innate aggressiveness of the human species, the allegedly Darwinian (more accurately, Herbert Spencerian) principle that human kind is biologically destined to engage in a struggle for survival, a struggle in which human groups, whole societies, battle with one another for the survival of the fittest. The more modern journalistic spin on that is to view the vicious civil conflicts now taking place in strange (for us) and exotic (for us) corners of the world such as Rwanda or Bosnia as "just" the settling of age-old "tribal" conflicts among peoples who have never gotten along, and never will.

The balance of the anthropological and historical evidence seems to say that these theories are wrong, and that it isn't nature, but nurture that is at the root of these "innate" conflicts. In fact, there is much evidence that says cooperation is a more "normal" (maybe even innate) form of human interaction than aggression and conflict. What these theories broadly argue is that it's the way people are raised or socialized (and maybe propagandized) in particular historical environments that largely determines whether they end up wanting to kill their neighbors or live with them in peace. This is as true for individuals whose personalities, shaped if not entirely determined by their families and communities, seem to propel them to anger and hatred as it is for whole peoples.

The evidence is pretty strong that people have to learn how to be violent. That's why the armed forces have basic training. One of the purposes of that "training," or resocialization from civilian life, is to overcome people's general reluctance to kill others. T. J. Stiles, author of *Jesse James, Last Rebel of the Civil War*, talks about the process he calls *violentization*, which he borrowed from Lonnie Athens's book *The Creation of Dangerous Criminals*. James grew up to be a very violent man, arguably a terrorist rather than the mythical social bandit. The process is: first, brutalization by an authority figure like a father or others, and the glorification of violence by friends. "Brutalization leads the subject to reject religious and cultural norms of civil behavior." Second, belligerence, as the subject makes an internal promise to use force to deal with any provocation. Third, the subject breaks through a "barrier" by actually inflicting pain on others. Finally, the development of a sense of immense power. Now the subject reacts with great force and violence to any small slight. In times of rapid social change and economic trouble, plenty of targets become available and our subject will suffer many injuries and, if surrounded by peers who suffer similarly (or think they do) and have weapons available, bloodshed will ensue. The James gang brutally shot unarmed civilians.

Most of the time hatred is directed toward an ethnically, including religiously and sometimes linguistically, and/or racially identifiable minority group that has become a scapegoat for some real or imagined evil. "Minority" groups exist only in the context of "majority." The context is that of a relationship involving differential access to some form of resource (often, but not only, economic). *Differential* means that one group is superordinate, and the other subordinate. Resources such as what? Jobs, status (or prestige), turf (geography; neighborhood), which is often attached to "values," meaning traditional ways of doing things—"The American Way of Life;" "Family Values;" "Morality;" "Religious Principles." Those are the combinations of variables that make up a person's "identity," which, in a rapidly changing world, is often challenged. America is no longer top dog in the world. African-Americans want their share of resources. Women are more economically independent. Divorce and illegitimacy rates climb. Immigrants are moving into the neighborhood. Fundamentalist or orthodox religion is undermined by science. Obscenity rules the airwaves. It's scary for the white man, especially when he is economically insecure on top of everything else.

Identifying a minority (or even a bunch of peaceniks or co-religionists who differ from you) as "the other" is the prerequisite to knowing your own identity. You have to know who they are not (they are not, or are different from, you), in order to know who you are. Why does identity seem so important to some people? Because identity is a kind of guarantee that the world isn't falling apart as fast as it seems to be. It's a security blanket, an island of safety, a defense mechanism. In short, it is based on the fear of losing something—jobs, neighborhood, prestige, values, tradition, power. The "other" becomes the source of this fear, and is hated. Hatred, then, is ultimately rooted in fear, although of course the hater does not understand this, and would vehemently deny that he, or she, is afraid of anything. Bluster and bullying, and, all too frequently, physical attack, are the cover for fear.

There are different circumstances in which intergroup hostility increases, or in other words turns into hate, because of these kinds of fears. Take two groups of people, let's call them A and B. The A's happen to dominate the society in terms of political and economic power, because they've been there the longest, and by and large are doing okay. Their ethnicity has historically given them a sense of superiority, even the poorer members of the group. The B's, an ethnic minority that practices a different method of worshipping God and happens to be of a darker complexion than the A's, is also doing okay economically. Traditionally they have been looked down on by the A's. As the economy improves, all boats rise. No problem. After a while the A's and the B's, who all go to the same schools and colleges, and work alongside each other in factories and offices, start to date each other, intermarry, and have babies that are mixed. Still no problem because everybody has access to economic and political resources, nobody is threatening anybody else's resources, and after a while the little matter of religious and "racial" differences turns out not to be that important. Love conquers all. The U.S. Census lists more than 2 million "multiracial" children for 2000, and I suspect many are the product of liaisons that happen in communities where resources are somewhat more equitably distributed between the "races" than in the rest of the country. About half of all Jews marry non-Jews, and that, too, takes place, most likely, in communities where both Jews and non-Jews are relatively secure and "mix" on relatively equal terms.

But let's suppose some of the A's, who have always dominated the society, suddenly aren't doing so well. Corporations are moving to Thailand. Jobs are disappearing. They are, or they believe they are, skidding downward. But the B's, who have perhaps been more prudent about investing their money, or have found secure economic niches in some businesses, are still doing okay. And some of them are doing better in schools and colleges than the A's, so they end up with some of the juicier jobs and the A's end up at the unemployment office. What happens then? The A's are likely to say, "They're getting breaks they don't deserve, why don't we get those breaks too?"

Or, conversely, the B's don't do so well in the first place because perhaps they don't speak English and don't have computer skills. So when the economy turns down they end up on the short end. And they don't seem to be able to get jobs because if the job market is tight, the A's are going to hire their friends and relatives, and the B's get left out. How are the B's going to react? Hostility will increase against the A's. How will the A's react to their reaction? The reaction is likely to be: "our group made it, why don't they work harder?" Even if both groups are poor, one is always poorer than the other. Logically, they should unite in common cause against the sources of their poverty (big business, perhaps?). But this unity is very often undermined by political opportunism at all levels, on both sides. Jobs are at stake, and when jobs are scarce, there will be trouble.

So the issue often boils down to a question of access to resources. If there are resources to go around (jobs, income, land, prestige, political clout), there may still be conflict, but it will be low-level. But if resources are, or become, scarce (which seems to be most of the time in most places nowadays), we get serious conflict. Why is that so hard to understand?

The reason it's so hard to understand is that people have been taught a lot of myths over their lifetimes. Some of these myths are hangovers from earlier times. The B's didn't just suddenly appear yesterday. They have a past, and so do the A's. They have histories (fact or fiction, in various mixes) that predispose them to dislike the other group when that becomes functional, that is, when there's a payoff such as protecting jobs. And even without those hangovers from past history, there are a few people in whose interest it is to play one group off against the other for various political and economic advantages. Some politicians play the "race card" to manipulate fears so they can get elected. Some employers play it to keep workers at each others' throats in order to prevent them from unionizing and asking for more money or benefits. And in a time of insecurity, people are looking for that "island of safety" to hang onto, and that island is their own precious "identity," their ethnicity, or race, or religion, or even their heterosexual identity, or some combination thereof, in opposition to folks who are not part of that "island," the "others" out there who are a threat, or are perceived to be a threat, which amounts to pretty much the same thing.

So the thesis here is that people, and groups of people, don't hate each other because it's in their genes as human beings, but because resources are tight, and they have no other way to understand that except to blame it on somebody else (usually with the eager help of some politicians, some of the media, and some parts of the economic power structure for which the manipulation of these insecurities is good business).

Now let's get real. We aren't talking about A's and B's, are we? We're talking about real groups in U.S. society and elsewhere, whites, African-Americans, Latinos, Native-Americans, immigrants of various backgrounds, Christians, Jews, Moslems, Hindus, etc. We are also talking about other kinds of differences between groups, not the least of which are gender and sexual preferences (gays and lesbians, and bi- and transsexuals). And physically-challenged or handicapped people. And although they are pretty invisible here, not so in Canada and European countries: Gypsies, more correctly called the Sinti and Roma people.

We, that is, the North American and Western European peoples, are pretty lucky even at that. We don't have civil wars between different groups of people within a country much anymore, although there continues to be violent conflict just short of civil war, as in Northern Ireland or the Basque area of Spain. Other folks are not so lucky, and the conflicts between their respective A's and B's (and, usually, third and other parties as well) have in recent years become major conflagrations, as groups of people who have previously been one-down compared to other groups in their particular country seek "national self-determination" in order to get out from under, even as that quest ends up subjugating still other groups, and turning their rivers red with their own and others' blood. All this in the name of patriotism, the flag, the race, the nation, the true faith, but underneath it all, for resources: land, water rights, capital, jobs, security for the family, and, hidden behind all that, fame, power, and profit for a handful of rulers.

What we have in Western countries is the retail version of that slaughter, at least so far. A few immigrants get burned out in some German town, another gets stomped to death in Oregon, there are assaults and even the murders of a handful of doctors performing abortions, some black kids in the "wrong" neighborhood, a Jewish kid in another "wrong" neighborhood, a few bombs here and there, no big deal, at least not until Oklahoma City. Some of that sounds racial or ethnic or religious. Some makes no sense from that angle, at least not directly, but even the Oklahoma City bombing, if we look closely, had something to do with somebody's insecurities, frustrations, lack of access to resources, and need to deal with the problem or to get even with the source of the problem (no matter how misconstrued and misdirected. More on this in chapter 5).

These incidents are not just isolated events attributable to a few nuts. There is, in the United States today (as in a number of other Western countries) a wave of pseudopopulism, a political backlash going on that proposes social policies that threaten to immiserate those who are already poor, pauperize the working class, and set one minority against the next and the white working class against all of them. It is a classic divide-and-conquer strategy that functions to strengthen capital and profit and promote greed. Movements ring a call (sometimes literally) to arms to another population of frustrated and marginal folk, a call that is clothed in the all-too-familiar garb of racism, anti-Semitism, homophobia, machismo, conspiracy theories, and superpatriotism.

These movements of the right, of fascism or proto-fascism if we want to call them by their right name, give meaning to people's lives, a meaning based on scapegoating some vulnerable group, and on false patriotism, on xenophobia, the fear and exclusion of others, all in the name of "values," "morality," "Americanism," and of course underneath all of those, the "sanctity" of the white race. These are the movements of growing numbers of the unsecure, who seek islands of safety in a rapidly changing and increasingly unsecure world. We know there is no safe haven in xenophobia, racism, and demagogic sloganeering, despite what some talk-show hosts seem to believe. We know that safety comes only from a world made secure by an educated citizenry in a democratically organized society. But the insecure, the marginals, don't know that, and don't trust our protestations. If we are to be convincing we must understand how to convince, which means that we must understand the movements we need to combat. But first we need to look at some of the ways individuals manage to convince themselves that hate is okay, that bigotry is acceptable, and that even violence against some scapegoat group is justifiable.

Denying Abuse: Tricks of the Trade

$\mathcal{O}$n July 13, 1942, a battalion of police attached to the German army in Poland was transported to a small town called Józefów, where they rounded up the 1,800 or so Jews who lived there, separated out the men, who were to be sent to a labor camp, took the remaining women and children to a nearby wood, and executed them.

Now for a different scenario: We are in a typical New Jersey suburb about fifty miles south of New York City. The homes are comparatively small, but each one has a bit of lawn, and perhaps a small garden in the rear. In the local high school about half the students are white, about one-quarter African-American, and the remainder divided among Latinos (Mexican-Americans, Puerto Ricans, Central Americans) and an increasing number of South Asians (children of Indian and Pakistani immigrants whose well-educated parents have come to take jobs in New Jersey's high-tech sector). Conflict between various ethnic groups within the student body, never totally absent, has now taken a new turn. The victims of harassment, bullying, and occasionally even violent bigoted attacks are not the African-Americans, as is often the case in suburban schools with a minority black population, or gays, as is also reported in such schools. Rather, it is the South Asians.

On March 3, 1991, in Los Angeles, an African-American man named Rodney King failed to stop when signaled by a police car. After police (there were twenty-five on the scene) finally succeeded in stopping the car and arresting King, he received fifty-six baton blows which resulted in eleven skull fractures, brain damage, and kidney damage. No police officers reported the incident.

In August 1997, the New York City police arrested a Haitian immigrant named Abner Louima outside a nightclub following an argument. On the way to the police station, while in handcuffs, he was allegedly beaten. At the station two officers shouted racist slogans, and one shoved a wooden toilet plunger handle into Louima's mouth and rectum. He was hospitalized for two months. No officer made a formal report of the event, and none intervened to stop the torture of this man.

In May 2004, the American public was apprised of a scandal involving the abuse and torture of Iraqi prisoners by American soldiers and contract workers at Abu Ghraib prison. Photographs taken by the perpetrators appeared in the press and on TV. In this case attempts were made by some soldiers to stop the offenses, and courts martial were instituted against some of the offenders.

How are we to understand these phenomena? Sociologists, among other experts, have come up with numerous answers to the question of what makes people ready to assault, torture, and murder others. In the case of the German police, military orders were followed sometimes reluctantly, sometimes not: the perpetrators had been "socialized" or indoctrinated in such a way that they would follow orders they regard as legitimate even when they ran contrary to the teachings of their religions or their own moral scruples. In police brutality cases it is often said that racism is key, and peer group pressure guarantees conformity and silence after the fact. For broader segments of the population it is said that economic insecurity, the increasing competition for fewer and fewer jobs for those with only high school diplomas, in short the struggle over resources, is a significant factor. But whatever the structural underpinnings, the apparent willingness of ordinary soldiers (not necessarily Nazis) to murder innocent civilians, or of police, including military police, to brutalize prisoners, or of students to express their prejudices and indeed act on them in sometimes violent ways, must in some measure be traceable to beliefs and attitudes that exist at home. For soldiers or police officers, beyond what attitudes parents may or may not have instilled in them by word or deed, their work environments, which often involve danger and fear, are more likely to promote than to inhibit violence against those who seemingly, and often actually, endanger them. Many Germans had been taught to fear Jews as conspirators seeking control of the world, or at best subversive of presumed German values and traditions.

In many situations involving anger and hate there often seems to be an undercurrent of fear about something, whether it involves physical danger, economic insecurity, or threats to one's status or standing, that overcomes the individual's sense of fair play, or the individual's willingness to say "no" to bad behavior, and this is reinforced by the peer group. The behavior of American GIs in the Abu Ghraib prison scandal in Iraq in 2003–2004 is perhaps only a recent extreme version of this phenomenon.

Or is it? Can all these instances of abuse be the work of a few "bad apples" in a larger barrel of decent people? Or is it the reverse, that there are often a few good apples in a barrelful of rotten people and then peer pressures turn some of them bad as well? Are these cases exceptions, or are they exceptions only because they came to be reported? Amnesty International tells us in its 2000 survey of 149 countries that "in the majority . . . there were credible allegations of torture or ill-treatment," and that in 125 countries security forces (police, military) tortured or ill-treated prisoners. There surely appears to be a shortage of empathy for "the other," the stranger, the immigrant (in the New Jersey example), and others who are perceived as deviant (including common criminals, political prisoners, members of minority groups, gays, in short just about anybody who does not fit the image of what the perpetrators of abuse see as legitimate members of the dominant ingroup).

These "others" are convenient targets onto which to project or displace blame and anger, what we often call scapegoating. This seems to be a common way of dealing with whatever malaise afflicts many people. Psychologists have been analyzing scapegoating for a very long time, and have suggested two underlying mechanisms: *Projection* is where we see in others (accurately or not) those inner strivings (especially sexual, the Freudians say) that are unacceptable in us. So we project onto another group our unacceptable laziness, greed, sexual licentiousness, those hidden desires that we more or less successfully repress in our daily lives. One analyst of homophobia has suggested that as long as we are frightened about our own secret (homosexual) desires, we will try to destroy those who are perceived to express those desires openly.

More important from the sociological perspective is the other kind of scapegoating: the *displacement* of blame for a problem from one place or person to another that is easier to identify, and easier to attack. "The system" is invisible, but the corner grocer or clothing store owner, especially if that person is of a different race or ethnicity, is not. It is easier to blame child abuse on the strange man with the raincoat (who is virtually nonexistent in statistical fact) than to confront the fact that the overwhelming majority of "missing children" are missing because they have been abducted by a spouse in a custody battle, or have run away from abusive homes. A necessary mechanism in this displacement is the negative stereotyping of the "other." Often these negative stereotypes are indeed projections: the African-American as sexually potent, the Jew as clever and sharp businesswise, the hippie as free from social constraints, the Irish (once upon a time) as drunkards, the Mexicans as lazy layabouts. Any and all of these people are blamed for whatever social ill currently dominates the headlines. Fact has nothing to do with it.

The vehemence of the opposition to gay marriage provides another example of the displacement mechanism. Many people fear gay marriage because they sense the frailties in their own marriages. They see, accurately enough, that the institution of marriage has been weakening. They believe, wrongly, that marriage as they understand it (male-female, one of each) is sacred, God-given, universal, and eternally fixed. They cannot see that they themselves, or perhaps more sociologically speaking, larger social forces that are not readily visible, are responsible for the changing nature of family structure, so they displace the blame onto gay marriage. If gay marriages are prevented, the sacred institution of marriage that is for them the very foundation of their identity will be preserved. Gay marriage is not just gay marriage. It is symbolic of something much more vast: the destruction of the very bedrock of Judeo-Christian civilization. Hence the ferocity of the attack.

Conspiracy theories play a role here, too: the idea that "the capitalist system" is responsible for unemployment is pretty vague; the idea that it's an international Jewish financiers' conspiracy is somehow more manageable, particulary if there already exists, in some segment of the population, a history of anti-Semitism. This history may be partly based on the reality that there are Jews who play exploitative roles in the community as "middleman minorities" for whatever historical reason. Middleman minorities, not just Jews, play the scapegoat role in many societies.

What scapegoats have in common is their political vulnerability in the society: they are a numerical minority with little if any clout (except for those conspiracy theories that pin the blame on that minority of mostly white Protestants who actually do dominate our social institutions—maybe some conspiracies are actually real!). Sometimes scapegoated minorities are better off than the majority of the "dominant" population: Jewish merchants/Polish peasants. Sometimes they are worse off: welfare moms/wage-earning moms. We envy those who are better off, and despise those who are worse off. In the former case we say, since they have what we don't have, there must be some secret reason for their advantage, namely, they are cheating, they are conspiring, they have secret networks. In the latter case we say, since they are worse off than we are, it is because they are not as hard-working, it is their own fault. The sociologists Richard Sennett and Jonathan Cobb, in their perceptive book *The Hidden Injuries of Class,* talk about how many working people deeply resent welfare recipients, even when they know the reasons that may force people onto the dole. Working people almost by definition make great sacrifices to keep families together and send children to school and, hopefully, on to higher education and upward mobility. "If there are people who have refused to make sacrifices, yet are subsidized by the state, their very existence calls into question the meaning of acts of self-abnegation." The welfare recipient, rather than the economy that limits workers' horizons, becomes the displaced object of hatred. Both better-off and worse-off scapegoats are keeping us down, the first because we, the deserving, are kept out of the game, the second because we are asked to pay for their undeserved support.

However, scapegoating does not explain how people give themselves permission to engage in and/or justify abusive, violent, and downright evil behavior including torture towards other human beings. In many instances, it only sets the stage: blame the immigrants for taking "our" jobs away; blame the Jews for our financial losses; blame gays and lesbians for the alleged collapse of family values. But in many other cases of abusive behavior, scapegoating is not really at issue. The Jews in some Eastern European shtetl are scapegoated because it is believed they are responsible for the financial ruin of the peasants, and then are attacked. The prisoners at Abu Ghraib prison are not being scapegoated particularly, although of course they are considered the enemy; they are being attacked because those in charge are able and willing to do so and are encouraged by their peers and the failure of their superiors to stop them.

As in the Abu Ghraib case, their superego mechanisms, a Freudian might say, their consciences, had gone AWOL and there was almost no one to remind them, no one who stepped in to say, "wait a minute, this is wrong, this is criminal," or even to warn, commonsensically, that eventually there might be consequences. In both cases, there was a "culture" that simply assumed there would be no consequences. Indeed, on the rare occasion when there is a "whistleblower," that person is often ostracized or even punished. One officer who later provided some information in the Abner Louima case had to be transferred to avoid retaliation from those in his precinct.

Whether based in scapegoating or not the question remains: How do victimizers justify and rationalize their behavior, and how do others excuse it? Given that all religions officially promote the principle of empathy, of identifying with the suffering, and that the vast majority of households claim some religious commitment if not actual affiliation, how is it that people are able to justify and rationalize this lack of empathy for "the other" and act in bigoted, violent ways, even to the extent of torture, toward those seen as "different" in whatever way?

People use a number of (unconscious) strategies to accomplish these justifications and rationalizations. They are of course unaware that these strategies are evasions because they cannot admit to themselves that what they are doing is wrong. They are abetted in these strategies by their upbringing (these strategies are learned, not innate), by the media, which promote these strategies through a choice of stories and imagery, by political misleaders, and even by the form and content of their education (especially their history courses and textbooks). These strategies are constantly reinforced by peers who participate in the behaviors that require justification, and by authority figures (role models) who condone these behaviors or indeed lead them.

These are the tricks of the trade: *trivialization, sanitization, relativization, blaming the victim, dehumanization,* and *I, the Jury.*

Here are some short definitions: *Trivialization* is minimizing the atrocious conduct that took place, making it out to be less than it was. Defense Secretary Donald Rumsfeld on Abu Ghraib: "What has been charged so far is abuse, which I believe technically is different from torture." *Sanitization* is another form of trivialization in which the act is cleaned up, whitewashed in a sense. In the TV series *Hogan's Heroes* a German prisoner-of-war camp is depicted as not much different from a summer camp for children, with the "counselors," as in many summer camp movies, merely incompetent buffoons. *Relativization* is a way of putting an event into a comparative context so that it is no worse than, or not nearly as bad as, what others have done. Secretary of State Colin Powell: "In war, these sorts of horrible things happen every now and again, but they're still to be deplored." In any case, Saddam Hussein's torturers were much worse. *Blaming the victim* is making victims responsible for their own abuse. The Abu Ghraib prisoners at one point rioted. Their GI guards were under great stress. Their (abusive) reaction was the natural result of the prisoners misbehaving. It was the guards' assignment to regain control by whatever means necessary. *Dehumanization* is defining the victim as less than human, as different (it helps when the victim is of a different color) and not part of the civilized family. This is ultimately the best way to rationalize abuse. Radio talk-show host Rush Limbaugh, in denying charges that the G.I. perpetrators at Abu Ghraib were "sick:" The prisoners are the ones who are "sick . . . perverted . . . dangerous . . . subhuman. They are the ones who are human debris." *I, the Jury* is when individuals decide that the law is inadequate, or too corrupted, to assure that justice will be done. The classic case is that of the lynch mob that forces its way into a prison and takes a prisoner out of jail and hangs him, sometimes after torture, to widespread applause, and the taking of souvenir photographs (or even the taking of body parts as souvenirs) to commemorate what is considered a justified action.

Let's look at these tricks of the trade in more detail, using a number of examples such as those mentioned above, but also including that ultimate abuse, the Holocaust.

Trivialization works this way: Almost all even moderately-informed people know about the Holocaust and do believe that the Nazis murdered six million-plus Jews and others deemed members of "inferior races." After all, there are hundreds of thousands of direct or indirect confirming witnesses and there is plenty of documentary evidence. Yet despite the evidence, a small part of the population (including even some masquerading as "academics") refuse to believe it (Holocaust deniers) or downplay it. The disbeliever asserts that the event could not have taken place, or if it happened, it could not have been as bad as depicted by the alleged victims. "Sure, several hundred thousand civilians were killed by the Germans. But that happens in wartime. It is not possible that six million Jews, and several millions of others, were murdered by a civilized people. In any case it is not physically feasible to carry out an enterprise of this magnitude."

In the Abu Ghraib incident, some people responding to news interviewers remarked of this torture that it was "no worse than fraternity hazing," that the prisoners were merely "humiliated," and not really hurt. U.S. officials repeatedly condemned the humiliation (or abuse) visited upon prisoners, carefully avoiding the term "torture" despite the evidence, and despite the fact that the prisoners' treatment met the definition of torture not only in international law but even according to military regulations. Defense Secretary Rumsfeld: "I'm not going to address the 'torture' word."

"Yes, the police beat King," said interviewees after the Rodney King incident. "But it was only to subdue an unruly prisoner, nothing particularly brutal, strictly within the prescribed rules." In the Abner Louima case, five officers were ultimately charged with crimes ranging from aggravated sexual abuse and first degree assault to covering up the incident. Yet Police Commissioner Howard Safir stated on several occasions that it was not a case of police brutality.

U.S. Supreme Court Justice Clarence Thomas was nominated for the position by President George H.W. Bush in 1991. Confirmation hearings before the Senate Judiciary Committee took place that fall. During the course of these hearings, a woman named Anita Hill, who had worked for Thomas in two government bureaus, came forward to charge that she had been the victim of his sexual harassment. She testified before the committee and provided considerable details. Thomas denied everything. Whether or not her charges were true remains a matter of some controversy even today. But that is not relevant to the issue of trivialization. Even many of those who found Hill's testimony credible trivialized it. In any number of interviews, with men in particular, the general sentiment was this: "Okay, Judge Thomas probably did say something to Professor Hill. But it is not imaginable that it was what she said, or even if he said it, it was a long time ago, in a different context, and he didn't mean much by it. It was just 'down-home courting.'" (The expression is taken from an op-ed piece by Professor Orlando Patterson, an African-American sociologist, *New York Times,* October 20, 1991.) Many Europeans thought that Hill's charges were blown out of all proportion because of our odd and hypocritical propensity to Victorian moralizing. What was the big deal?

Another way to trivialize the issue is to impute bad motives to the complainant. This is not the same as blaming the victim for the abuse; it is an attempt to discredit the story. The Holocaust is a propaganda maneuver instigated by the international Zionist conspiracy; King was fully in control and maneuvered police into over-reacting so he could pose as a martyr and victim of police brutality, and anyway the bleeding-heart liberal media blew it out of proportion in order to discredit the police. Similarly, Anita Hill's sexual harassment charge was contrived by slick lawyers in the pay of "politically-correct" liberals in order to prevent Clarence Thomas, a conservative, from being nominated to the Court. In the case of Anita Hill, even better, she was avenging herself for a rejection. And, of course, we need to "get over" the Abu Ghraib and similar incidents: these are merely political attacks on the president by Democrats, and deflect attention from winning the war. Generals belong in the field, not in Washington facing committee investigations.

Another form of trivializing an act is to sanitize it, to clean it up, to make it look less bad than it really is, or was, or to reinterpret it to make it benign. The media are often responsible for doing this, perhaps because the truth is assumed to be too brutal, so awful that we need to deny it. In any case it is surely not entertainment. Or there is a vested interest, materially or psychologically, in denial, trivialization, and sanitizing. So the media sanitize many problems: you, the responsible individual, can stop smoking if you want to (it is not an industrial problem); if you get cancer it is because you chose to smoke, or to eat unhealthy foods; you are responsible for pollution and can stop it with a bit of recycling (it too is not an industrial problem); you are responsible for your own obesity—all this adds up to the American creed of individual responsibility, which sanitizes the larger responsibilities of corporations or government, or indeed the wider culture.

We often get sanitized accounts of widespread problems before the full truth about, say, starvation in Somalia, the extent of AIDS-inflicted suffering, the degree of homelessness, the murder or disappearance of large numbers of people in the course of an "ethnic cleansing," or the work of death squads, surfaces. Governments debate about whether to call armed attacks and large-scale murders of civilians in the Sudan genocide, or merely ethnic cleansing. And when the truth does come out, we minimize it by attributing the event to some act of God or nature that we cannot affect. It is, after all, painful to confront such suffering particularly when we can do little about it. We rationalize our helplessness by saying that it's exaggerated, or, in the case of famine, that it is the result of an inevitable drought, even though that is not true.

Sometimes a great deal of energy is spent after a horrifying event to try to sanitize it in an attempt to escape blame. People get into arguments about numbers of casualties. Were there really 6 million Jews killed by the Nazis? Maybe there were only 2 million? 250,000? Was Hiroshima actually a military base filled with soldiers? Was Dresden really an important railway hub? How many soldiers constitute a military base? Was it okay to kill 200,000 civilians because there were as many soldiers there? Only 50,000 soldiers? Not okay if there were fewer than 50,000 soldiers? Did Stalin starve 5 million farmers to death? Only 2 million? You can see how insane that form of sanitization can become.

Let's look at a classic example of media sanitization. The depiction of the POW camp in *Hogan's Heroes* is patently fraudulent. It utterly distorts history, and teaches a very false lesson, namely, that it all wasn't so bad. But it was so bad. In Eugen Kogon's study *The Theory and Practice of Hell* he describes the lot of 167 British pilots and 43 British and French underground workers. No funny POW camp for them. Sixteen of the 43 were hanged on September 9, 1944. On October 4, 1944, twenty of the officers were shot. And so on. *Hogan's Heroes* not only promulgates a lie, but turns the Germans not into what they really were, mostly pretty normal human beings many of whom did some awful things, but into clowns, into inferior national stereotypes, that is, into the victims of television's own brand of racism. How ironic that the public should be subjected to a portrait of a group that practiced the most extreme racism, and have them painted as a nationality of fools, thus helping turn the viewers into racists themselves.

A third common strategy is to downgrade the act by relativizing it. Yes, there was a Holocaust. But everybody did something like that. Certainly the Communists, from Stalin to Pol Pot. And even we did it: think of Dresden, of Hiroshima and Nagasaki. We are all guilty, therefore no one is guilty. This is a particularly useful strategy when it comes to war and conquest. The injustice of enslaving and murdering large numbers of Native Americans, for example, during the early years of the Spanish conquest, is made easier by demonstrating that the Aztecs, too, were cruel, with their human sacrifice, their enforced labor for the victims of their conquests, etc. There is a symmetry, too, in the depiction of Vietcong cruelties during the Indochina war, though the Rambo films don't even bother with that approach: the enemy is responsible for all the cruelty so that whatever we did to them, they had it coming. This was also used as one of the justifications for the bombing of civilian targets in World War II, including the use of the A-bomb against Japan. After all, it is true that Japanese soldiers committed massive atrocities against civilian populations, as well as captured soldiers.

It is interesting that the Japanese use a similar form of relativization in order to escape any sense of guilt for their role in World War II. After all, were they not cruelly bombed by the Americans? A more recent form of relativization is the widespread public attention devoted to the issue of Germans displaced from their lands by the shifting of borders after World War II. Surely a calamity for them, but hardly a decent way to relativize the issue of the Holocaust. And we all know about Saddam Hussein's murders and tortures, in the very same prison that became the site of American scandals.

The facts of history become distorted or dismissed. The massive bombardments in Vietnam, including the North, the genocidal impact of Europeans on the peoples of the Americas in the half-century after 1492, the utterly wasteful and useless destruction of German and Japanese cities that had little or no military value, these events do not weigh as we attempt to relativize through the depiction of "paired cruelties."

We are absolved of guilt for an act if everyone else does it or has done it. If every police department engages in some police brutality, if every man hassles a woman at some time, then no one is guilty. Police need to use force to control criminal elements. Men need to express their sexual prowess. It's human nature, it's part of our culture. Therefore Judge Thomas is no more guilty than his jury of white male senators including Strom Thurmond (surely that is true!). Thomas, incidentally, used a form of relativization when, in response to Hill's charges and the hearings that probed them, he called the proceedings "a high-tech lynching." He used this again when he stated that he would "not provide the rope for my own lynching or for further humiliation." So, compared to her charges even if true, "lynching" him for it was surely worse. Why pick on Thomas, the Germans, the LAPD? Why pick on American GIs? We are all guilty of something.

Another strategy is to blame the victim for the abuse by asserting that there must be a reason a group or person gets victimized. What is that reason? They must have done something. Where there's smoke, there's fire. Jews, after all, are stereotypically known to be conniving cheats, financial manipulators, and unpatriotic (objective facts play virtually no role in undermining prejudiced attitudes). Who can blame the clean-living Germans for trying to control the Jews? As for Rodney King, he was probably on drugs, he should have followed orders and stayed still. On the witness stand one of the officers stated they beat King because he failed to follow instructions. Likewise, Professor Hill must have done something to instigate Judge Thomas, as is often said of rape victims: perhaps she made a play for him, perhaps her skirt was too short. As for AIDS victims, it's God's punishment for sin in one way or another: being gay, using dirty needles, or, in any event, not being careful. It is as American as apple pie to blame the poor for being poor, welfare recipients for being on welfare, the unemployed for failing to find work.

The outbreak of gay-bashing (including the backlash against gay marriage) in recent years goes beyond a mere lack of empathy, of course, but also fits this category. Why gays? In this rapidly changing world male domination is under fire from several quarters. As women enter the labor force in increasing numbers and proportions, including into some of its better-paid layers, the income gap between men and women gradually narrows—not because women are so much better off, but because men are getting worse off and are skidding downward. The economic reality is that many men are being forced out of the labor force and their dominant role in the family is thereby threatened. Meanwhile the gay and lesbian movement for equal rights has come out into the open (and many gays and lesbians out of the closet as a result). A degree of sexual insecurity or ambivalence, always present but usually kept latent, gets mixed into this brew of economic (job) insecurity and social (family) insecurity and becomes more overt with the literal presence of gays and lesbians living openly in the community. Nowadays bigots find it more difficult, at least in the United States, to openly attack Jews, African-Americans, or immigrants, although of course this is also done. Bigots need an easier victim group, a smaller minority that can also be vilified on the basis that it is a menace to our youth and is corrupting the morality of the nation (much the same thing was said by the Nazis about the Jews). Also, bystanders are less likely to go to the assistance of gays or lesbians, lest they be found guilty by association. If the victims had stayed "in the closet" nothing bad would have happened; they are blamed for the violence against them because they are out, just as African-Americans were frequently blamed for the violence against them because they were out of line—or "uppity." Had they continued to behave according to protocol, they would not have been lynched.

A second aspect of blaming the victim is to absolve the perpetrator of responsibility because the victim didn't fight back. Why didn't Hill tell him where to get off? Why didn't she quit? What is the matter with her? Why didn't the Jews fight back (more)? To the degree that the victim can be depicted as weak, the victim can be discounted, especially in a society like ours that is based on an individualistic, macho tradition, even a vendetta mentality, as justified in so many movies. Generally gays are perceived to be weak (like women) by definition, but for some reason, while it isn't supposed to be chivalrous to beat up a woman, it is perfectly okay to beat up gays. In point of fact the former are constantly getting beaten "when they get out of line," and since the latter are by definition out of line. That's why chivalry isn't even an issue when it comes to gay bashing. Chivalry is only when people stay in their place. People are not supposed to fight back whey they are attacked for "getting out of line." It is the bigot who defines what that line is, of course.

It seems to be out of line when victims fight back against duly constituted authority, like our boys in blue, the nice guys who help kids cross at street corners and who protect us against the rioting hordes. Some people thought Rodney King was fighting back, and he shouldn't have done that. He should have followed orders and since he presumably didn't, what happened was his own fault. He got what he deserved.

The bigot is able to "discount" or "deny" abuse by using the above strategies, usually in combination, even when they are logically in contradiction. If everybody does it, after all, we are admitting that something happened. But it helps to be able to say that what did happen wasn't so bad, and anyway the victim brought it on her/himself, and in addition I'm on the side of important and powerful people.

Perhaps the most important trick of the trade is to dehumanize the victim, as Rush Limbaugh did in describing the Abu Ghraib prisoners. Most of the time this is done by negative stereotyping: depicting the victim as possessing bad, undesirable characteristics that run counter to the dominant culture. These negatives can run the gamut from being too dumb (genetically inferior) to too smart (too conniving, as with Jews). The entire project that we term *racism*, in which one "race" is deemed superior to another, is the framework in which most forms of dehumanization take place. The Greeks thought the Persians were savages, and to one extent or another every side in every war has tried to dehumanize the enemy even when both sides were basically of the same "race" or even ethnic makeup. The treatment of Native-Americans by European-background settlers, even to the point of hunting them like animals, could not have been possible without the idea that the victims were subhuman.

Here is Roger Casement, a leading figure of Irish republicanism: "The African savage . . . delights in bloodshed, whether it be on the field of battle or in human sacrifice" and, from Brazil, "the 'Brazilian' is the most arrogant, insolent and pigheaded brute in the world." In 1910 he described Brazilians as a "loathsome people. . . . A mixture of Jew and Nigger and God knows what; altogether the nastiest human black pudding the world has yet cooked in her tropical stew pot." (From *The New York Review of Books,* May 27, 2004). Casement, we must remember, is considered an enlightened human being.

The enlightened have been involved in the dehumanization project all along. This history is closely intertwined with the "scientific" study of race from the late nineteenth century through the Nazi period, and is associated with the "scientific" field called eugenics. Eugenics is dedicated to the proposition that genetically inferior human beings should be prevented from procreating, and that a better human race (traditionally white Anglo-Saxon) can be developed by careful breeding. This was a major social movement until the late 1930s, supported financially by established American foundations and politically by many important figures.

One would think this approach was finally laid to rest after the war against Nazism. One would be wrong. The issue of alleged racial differences in intelligence continues to absorb the energies not only of right-wing fanatics but even of some scientists. In the mid-1960s Arthur Jensen, a University of California psychologist, concluded after reviewing what he considered the relevant scientific literature that blacks were genetically less intelligent than whites. The article summarizing his view was published in the respected *Harvard Educational Review* in 1969. But even more recently, a book titled *The Bell Curve* (1994), co-authored by Harvard psychologist Richard Herrnstein and the conservative intellectual Charles Murray, made headlines by claiming that inequality in the United States is rooted in differences in "cognitive ability" as measured by IQ tests. Their conclusion is to oppose the kinds of social reforms that are intended to level the playing field as useless: since cognitive ability is fixed by genetic inheritance, reforms will do no good. Of course what is at issue is *racial* differences, although the argument can also be used to explain *class* differences. It is interesting that many of the authors and publications relied on by Herrnstein and Murray were sponsored by a right-wing think tank called the Pioneer Fund, which was founded in the 1930s to promote eugenicism. *The Bell Curve* was thoroughly reviewed in both lay and professional publications and it is safe to say that the overwhelming opinion of the work was negative. The book was generally dismissed as both scientifically flawed and politically motivated. As William H. Tucker concludes in *The Science and Politics of Racial Research*, "Although the obsession with racial differences has contributed absolutely nothing to our understanding of human intellectual processes, it has performed continuing service as support for political policies—and not benign ones. The imprimatur of science has been offered to justify, first, slavery and, later, segregation, nativism, sociopolitical inequality, class subordination, poverty, and the general futility of social and economic reform."

It is wartime that brings out the worst kinds of dehumanization. In World War I it was the bestial Huns. They were replaced by the bloodthirsty Japs of World War II, and almost needless to say, the Nazis turned racism into a genocidal project in which even Slavs were considered an inferior race. Their Japanese allies were labeled "honorary Aryans" but real Nazis probably knew it was only for diplomatic reasons. Whoever the enemy, it is easier to kill them if they can be depicted as savage, less than fully human, or at best members of an inferior civilization.

The long history of American vigilantism provides us with many examples of the "I, the Jury" syndrome. Richard Maxwell Brown, in an anthology called *Violence in America,* defines it as "the tradition in which organized, extralegal movements take the law into their own hands." Obviously individuals do this as well. It is the rationale that is significant. It is, or is perceived to be, in support of community values at a time when law enforcement is seen as incapable of doing so. Forms of vigilantism include lynch mobs, the actions of the Ku Klux Klan or similar groups (possibly resulting in a lynch mob), various guerrilla activities before, during, and after the Civil War, particularly in Missouri and Kansas in support of the Confederacy and its proslavery ideas (the so-called social bandit Jesse James was involved in some of this), but also underground pro-labor movements such as the Molly Maguires in the coal fields of Pennsylvania. Arguably, the assassinations of presidents Abraham Lincoln,

James Garfield, William McKinley, and John F. Kennedy were the work of people who believed their deaths would serve the interest of the country, or at minimum would right some perceived wrong.

We now have a better idea of how people rationalize their lack of empathy. But why is it so weak in the first place, usually in contradiction to their religious heritage? It seems that the "functions" of prejudice and bigotry outweigh the guilt that ought to go with them. These "functions" include maintaining some secure identity (as white, a man, a heterosexual, an ethnic of whatever kind, a neighbor, a Christian, a patriotic American, etc.) in a rapidly changing and uncertain world that, overall, doesn't make much sense anymore. Even more important, it is a world that is challenging all the traditional perquisites that used to go with being white, male, etc. Scarce resources are about more than jobs and money (though those are extremely important). They also involve prestige or being respected (that is, recognized as superior), turf or being able to maintain a homogeneous neighborhood (that is, keeping others out), and values, which usually means doing things in the traditional way (that is, maintaining old-fashioned white supremacist "race relations," patriarchal family patterns, the comfort of "normal" heterosexuality etc.). There is also the quintessentially American value of individualism, which is linked to the work ethic: poverty is the fault of the poor (blaming the victim) because they allegedly do not work hard to find and keep jobs, unlike the rest of us. The work ethic, the ethic of individualism, it is widely believed, is being undermined by the state's coddling of criminals and its lax welfare policies, which in any case are useless in ameliorating inequality if one believes the eugenicists.

Finally, there are the threats to the political structures that have in the past functioned to protect these interests and values, threats that come both from domestic dissenters and foreign governments that in recent years have challenged American policy. As this fabric is shaken and undermined, bigotry, the opposite of empathy, becomes something solid to hold onto, an island of safety. When manipulated by political misleaders, and supported by authorities such as the police or military, bigotry translates into violence. This is the first thing to understand as we confront the obstacles on the road to bettering human relations.

· 3 ·

And the Oppressed Get Screwed:
Observations on the
Relationship of Politics and Sex

We know that language expresses how people feel about themselves and others. As we explore the way bigotry works, we observe that when one group denigrates another, the language of denigration, of "put-downs," becomes part of the process of hatred, bigotry, and victimization, and consequently part of the process of discrimination against the victims of bigotry.

It is fascinating, disturbing, and to some people odd, but it a fact that the language of "put-downs" and the language of sex (and sometimes other bodily functions) are closely interrelated. Even the term "put-down" is sexual, for that matter. There is, in other words, a connection between the victimizer-victim power relationship and sex (which is also about power), and this is reflected in language.

The connection between bigotry and victimization on the one hand, and the sexual dimension of human life on the other, has been observed by a handful of social scientists and social philosophers for some years. Writing in the 1930s, the radical German psychologist Wilhelm Reich argued that the fascist mentality was related to the suppression of sexuality. Other philosophers and social scientists such as Herbert Marcuse and Norman O. Brown, to mention just a few, have argued that political liberation was impossible without sexual liberation. The Mexican writer Octavio Paz has pointed to the sexual imagery of oppression. The African-American former radical and ex-con Eldridge Cleaver elaborated on the relationship between white oppression of blacks and the nature of sexual relations within, and between the races back in the '60s. The feminist writer Kate Millet has described the oppressive function of the treatment of women in even avant-garde literature. It has become a widely discussed, if not widely accepted, axiom that political relationships (that is, those that have to do with the distribution of power between individuals and groups)

23

are often perceived in sexual terms, and that in turn sexual relations, the relations of the sexes to each other both outside of bed and in, are political in nature (that is, involve relations of power, superordination and subordination, relations between oppressor and oppressed). Nowadays this axiom has also come to be applied to relationships among gays, and more broadly to the interaction between straights and gays (in the sense that one socially defined group oppresses the other, and that this oppression is laced with sexual overtones and undertones).

In social psychology the pioneering work of Gordon Allport, Abram Kardiner and Lionel Ovesey, John Dollard, and William Grier and Price Cobbs, again to mention only a few, has been basically in this tradition, while focusing on "race relations." Similarly, the writings of Frantz Fanon, a West Indian psychiatrist working during the Algerian revolution, and Albert Memmi, a Tunisian Jew living in France, elaborated this issue in terms of colonialism.

Sociology on the other hand has not paid much attention to this topic, perhaps because it is not readily subject to the kind of rigorous methodology that contemporary sociology likes to believe is at the heart of its scientific pretensions. Perhaps, too, it has something to do with the fact that the "sociology of oppression" is a dangerous area. It is one thing for philosophers, poets, and novelists, or even psychologists, to speak of such matters, for they deal with fiction, or what happens in individuals' heads. It is another for people who supposedly deal with social systems to begin to get at the heart of the matter.

In this chapter we will look at a set of relationships between victimization and sex to see how this works. We are going to set forth a series of propositions, look at some illustrative material, and then examine how this material strengthens, raises questions about, or otherwise helps us understand these propositions.

1. The extreme of oppression is involuntary sexual use and abuse, including rape and castration.

Castration has been the common lot of rebels going back to the peasant wars of the Middle Ages, slaves transgressing racial caste lines, slave revolt leaders, postbellum blacks crossing caste lines, union organizers on occasion. (to cite only a few documented instances). The ultimate torture used by, for example, the French during the uprising against them in Algeria, Batista in pre-Castro Cuba, Argentine generals, or, only in a somewhat less awful way, U.S. troops involved in the Abu Ghraib scandal has been, and remains, the abuse of the genitals of both men and women in the service of the oppressor's politics, primarily to strike fear into the hearts of potential rebels (the abused are often released, either dead or alive, to serve as examples) but also in the vain hope of extracting information. Under Hitler a variety of experiments were conducted on concentration camp inmates involving their sexual organs, not to speak of the exploitation of both men and women for sexual purposes directly, less as a deterrent than as a component of a racist, genocidal version of eugenics.

The use of castration as a "pacifying" mechanism is related to its presumed function of turning the aggressive male into a person more like a passive female. The *Random House Dictionary of the English Language* (College Edition, 1969), for example, defines *castrate:* "to womanize, subdue, pacify, make ruly (also use for sexual purposes as a woman, e.g. in Arab countries). Further, castration serves to take the punch, as it were, out of things. Thus, in subdefinition number three, the dictionary continues: "to deprive (a book, a text, etc.) of effect or import by deleting certain parts; expurgate."

Historically, psychoanalysis has posited that the fear of castration performs a vital function in the socialization of the male child. In Freudian theory the small boy is said to resolve the Oedipus complex (his incestuous love for his mother) through the fear of castration. This forces him to renounce the (unconscious) wish to possess his mother, and he comes to accept the authority of his father, and through him, the authority of society itself. Extending this line of reasoning to a critique of capitalism, Wilhelm Reich argued that this fear functions to maintain the bourgeois family within the framework of the patrifocal, patriarchal capitalist system.

The importance to men in many societies of having "balls," regardless of whatever cultural or psychosocial reason there may be for this, means that men suffer a psychic castration, as it has been described, when they fail, for whatever reason, to live up to the male sex stereotype. Those who don't prove their masculinity in the various ways a culture has told them it must be done, lack "balls." This translates into violence when men feel their masculinity has been challenged. Whether it is the "Southern code of honor" or the "Northern code of the streets," as psychiatrist Aaron Beck writes in *Prisoners of Hate,* the value systems that emphasize receiving respect and retaliating when diminished or "dissed" leads to high rates of violent behavior, and, he argues, to the high homicide rate among Southern whites (and presumably Northern urban gang members).

This argument is occasionally heard as a rationale for keeping African-American women from positions of leadership on the ground that African-American men already suffer too much psychic castration in this racist society to permit women a "one-up" position compared to them. Another version of this fear of strong women is when men use the expression "castrating bitch" to denote a woman who in some way has "put them down" or is seen as threatening to "one-up" them. Freudians would not have a difficult time figuring out what putting someone down, or being one-up, is really all about.

For women, castration takes the form of clitorectomy. There is a long history of justifying such procedures on the ground that it will "tame," that is, excise (!) unruly passions, hence they perform a social control function.

A common fear among many oppressed groups is that of physical attack, but the more severe version of this fear is that of sexual molestation by members of an oppressor group without the possibility of defense or retribution. This is a common theme in the literature of African-Americans. Fanon discusses a similar phenomenon in his analysis of Algeria under French domination. Prisoners of many kinds, both men and women, report fear of sexual attack by jailers or stronger inmates, a fear that is entirely based on reality. One of the reasons given by the homeless for preferring the streets to shelters is their fear of sexual attack.

Today rape has become a political issue as significant for women as, historically, lynching was for African-Americans prior to the 1950s. This is so obvious and so widely reported that further discussion here is unnecessary. Gays and lesbians likewise report a fear of sexual abuse, often combined with physical beatings, from police, citizens, racketeers, and blackmailers, as the second greatest danger of living in the gay/lesbian culture (AIDS having supplanted it at number one since the 1980s).

Involuntary sexual use and abuse of course extends beyond the extremes of rape and castration. It is now widely understood that sexual objectification, the dehumanizing or depersonalization of women (mostly, though also some men) by turning them into cosmetic objects, is another dimension of oppression. Hence the anger of so many feminists at the Miss America contests. But it is also understood among women in general and among the women of the working class and of oppressed minority groups in particular that sexuality is a commodity that can be used to manipulate the male oppressor (including husbands and lovers) in order first to survive, second to assure survival and a better status for one's children, and third to obtain a decent or at least bearable standard of living. Many nineteenth century potboilers were replete with stories of working girls getting jobs in a "meat market" atmosphere, and that theme persists today in many of the current soaps.

The irony in this is that oppressive culture has put woman into a self-fulfilling bind: the fact that she is socially and economically oppressed is both a cause and a consequence of her sexual objectification. To enable herself to survive, she manipulates her sexuality, commodifies it; in turn this enables men to not take her seriously since she doesn't look like a serious person, e.g., Eleanor Roosevelt. This cycle serves to maintain women in a set of subordinate roles that are inherently oppressive because they socialize women into false social roles not of their making, to respond to a social setting in which the authentic personality is unable to function. The woman is never quite sure (or, perhaps, is altogether too sure) about the real reason a man wants her. Similarly, a gay man wonders whether his partner is interested in him "only for my skin," and the interracial or interethnic date thinks something rather similar (this point was conveyed quite convincingly in the Spike Lee film *Jungle Fever*).

Sexual attractiveness becomes an instrument with which the woman, gay, ethnic minority, "working girl," concentration camp or prison inmate, or other, manipulates the sexual user, or oppressor, in order to obtain favors—repeated dates, marriage, money, services, tips, or, in concentration camps, life itself. Prostitution is merely the most obvious example of selling sex; political literature (especially of the left, going back to the *Communist Manifesto*) is filled with references to the idea that, at least in Western society, marriage itself is merely a covert form of prostitution, and is therefore part of the same manipulatory, false role-playing, hence oppressive, game.

Paradoxically, although sexual objectification (which is implicitly or explicitly a form of prostitution) is highly valued in this society when women use it to confirm their one-down place, it is used as a negative when women get "uppity." Women who aspire to positions of power may not be "sexy" lest they be accused of manipulating their sexuality, hence acting slutty. Either way, whether she stays in her place or attempts to compete, the sexually attractive woman is not taken seriously.

Another potential use of sex is when demagogues play the "sexual corruption" card in attempts to discredit liberal ideas. President George H.W. Bush's Vice-President Dan Quayle was obsessed with the unmarried single mother (hence sexually corrupt) Murphy Brown in a TV sitcom. But this was a mild example: racists of all types, ranging from Hitler to some fringe black nationalists, have attributed at least part of the problems of their particular group to sexual corruption that takes the form of miscegenation, or race-mixing. Second only in nightmarish symbolism to the American KKK mentality to "Niggers with guns" (as a Black Panther Party member once put it) is the image of African-American men in the company of white women.

The tragic consequences of oppression insofar as the sexual dimension is concerned are twofold: first, as we see, sexual use and abuse is used to sustain oppressive systems. But equally tragic is the fact that oppressed people rape (and otherwise assault) each other more than they rape and assault members of the oppressor group, and that this is true cross-culturally (c.f. Fanon). This form of "in-group aggression," which fits into the frustration-aggression thesis, suggests that the frustrations associated with being oppressed result in behavior that is at times the mirror image of the oppressor's behavior. Hip-hop lyrics that talk openly about rape and other violence to women seem to come out of a misogynistic mentality that is only a step removed from the actual act. It is generally regarded as music that arose from within the African-American underclass, a classic case of (verbal) in-group aggression.

Finally, there is the use of rape as a weapon of war, either during military operations to demoralize an enemy or after a war to take vengeance on a conquered enemy. From the Old Testament (Lamentations and Zechariah, for example), where the Hebrews are both victims and perpetrators, to very recent events in Bosnia and Rwanda, mass rapes by soldiers or paramilitaries have been committed in the course of war. Although it is often assumed that such acts are random, carried out by a few bad actors, or part of the spoils of war as in a number of biblical cases (where rape is sometimes combined with kidnapping and slavery, a familiar combination even without war), it is clear that in many instances mass rape has been a deliberate policy organized by the military as a weapon of war. In the 1990s Serbian troops used rape to force Muslim women to flee their homes, and to demoralize Bosnian Muslim soldiers. The rape of Nanking (Nanjing) in China by Japanese troops in 1937 and 1938 is also well documented. Following their occupation of Germany, Soviet troops raped vast numbers of German women in part in retaliation for the atrocities committed by the Nazis on Soviet soil.

2. The oppressed see their political position in sexual terms; they often see their sexual position in (latently) political terms. The oppressor also sees his (her) position in these terms.

The imagery about the oppressive relationship is a sexual one for both the oppressed and the oppressor. Octavio Paz in *The Labyrinth of Solitude* spends some time discussing the Mexican use of the verb "*chingar*," which, he points out, is not necessarily a synonym for the sexual act. However, "*Chingar* . . . is to do violence to another. The verb is masculine, active, cruel: it stings, wounds, gashes, stains. And it provokes a bitter, resentful satisfaction. . . . (T)he idea of violence rules darkly over all the meanings of the word." Similarly, in American English, a statement of defiance takes the form of "up yours," "fuck you," and similar terms. Victory, even a financial coup, takes the form of "I screwed him (her)" and the like. Political attitudes toward women take the form of the famous statement by a black nationalist, "the position of women in the movement is prone;" or defeat: "I've been had, screwed, fucked over, put down." Sexual terms are often related, as Paz also points out, to fecal terms: "Nobody's going to mess over me any more;" "he's an asshole" (especially popular in German). Even the once popular and joyful "sock it to 'em" and former President Nixon's request on a TV comedy show, "sock it to me" is sexual and often accompanies a vicarious pleasure at a popular figure "giving it" to an unpopular one. What can "it" be? For straight, homophobic males, "it" is the ultimate humiliation of the weak: it is to be the victim of the anal intercourse that is associated with the female partner in what is the ultimate in sexual corruption (even more corrupt than miscegenation, and subject to similar kinds of violent attack): homosexual intercourse. One has been "womanized," truly "fucked over," and what could be worse?

Seeing the sexual position in political terms is more complex. Sometimes sexual myths or alleged myths are seen as rationalizations for political oppression. For example, the "myth of the vaginal orgasm" has been described as Freud's rationalization for giving primacy in the sexual act to the man, to accompany his economically superior position in the family, and to justify that superiority. Various myths of female attributes such as emotionalism, infantilism, softness, even manual dexterity, are used as rationalizations for unequal treatment in the workplace. A manager of a Third World sweat shop is quoted in the documentary film *Double Day*: "They have smaller fingers, can do this kind of work (assembly of small engines) better." If women (and in the area of racial stereotypes African-Americans, Latinos, Jews, and so on) are sexually uncontrollable, irrational, childlike, and hedonistic, obviously they cannot be permitted significant decision-making power in modern technological society.

Similar myths are promoted concerning university students in order to justify their exclusion from participation in personnel, curricular, and other decision-making roles. The myth that the childlike person is too emotional and hedonistic (sexual, drugged-out, unable to postpone gratification) to take care of her/himself is an obvious rationalization for paternalism.

This is not negated by the use of sex and sexiness to sell products, or that in advertising, a product is associated with the image of a powerful, sexy person (usually male, as in the old Marlboro tobacco ads). In virtually every case, the image is one in which sex is under control. The powerful person is one who controls her/his sexuality, who is in command of it, and of the people being impressed (manipulated) by that sexuality which is derived, of course, from the product. Everyone in the room (of the opposite sex) is turned into a simpering idiot by the sexual power exuded by the product, applied to the hero or heroine, who is usually depicted as smiling benignly down at all those who have been turned into jelly by a whiff of the tobacco, perfume, deodorant, or toothpaste.

A corollary is that the oppressor needs to identify certain groups (possibly all subordinate groups) with a myth of uncontrolled or deviant sexuality as a rationale for introducing methods of controlling them. "Welfare reform" is an example: welfare mothers are alleged to be sexually irresponsible (having too many children out of wedlock), and therefore we need to control that by denying payment for additional children. The fact that welfare mothers do not, as a general rule, have a lot of children, and that this particular "reform" has had no effect on birthrates, is irrelevant.

Seeing women, blacks, or others as mythical sexual beings is functional in at least two senses: by a process of negative association it sets "proper" (repressed) sexual behavior up as the approved norm. The mythologized group thus serves as an aid in "boundary maintenance." Proper sexual behavior, which was traditionally linked to postponing sex until marriage, is a component of a more general postponement of gratification, which is the key ingredient of the Protestant ethic. This in turn leads to saving and investment, the key to the development of early capitalism according to the German sociologist Max Weber and many others (Benjamin Franklin among them, although he apparently was rather flexible about postponing his own sexual gratification). Improper sexual behavior (particularly having children out of wedlock) is said to be a major threat to the American family and way of life, hence few if any politicians will fail to condemn it.

All the worse if a politician steps over the boundary. Although divorce is now acceptable, should the spouse reveal some sexual peccadillo as a cause, the political career is over. Only a very few politicians have dared to reveal that they are gay and have survived politically. New Jersey's Governor James McGreevey resigned in August 2004 after revealing that he was "a gay American."

The myth of uncontrolled or inappropriate sexuality affords the proper, sexually repressed oppressor with a vicarious way of expending sexual energies. The fascination of many people with the misadventures of any given Hollywood star from Woody Allen to Michael Jackson is an example of this. Hippies ("long-hairs") used to perform a similar function for the system, perhaps accounting for the vicious treatment meted out to them by those guardians of the straight world, the police. Today, hip-hop or rap musicians have displaced hippies as the major sexual demons. It is groups that symbolize (stereotypically, not in reality for the most part) the myth of free floating, uninhibited sexuality, especially when they are also minorities, that seem to receive the harshest treatment from law enforcement agencies, who are, after all, in charge of boundary maintenance, a.k.a. protecting the dominant culture from invasion by the savage hordes. The inconsistency in this is that the enforcers of boundaries from time to time themselves engage in sexual practices that society officially frowns on. Sexual abuse, torture, and rape by security forces are often rationalized as necessary to keep other people "in line," that is, cognizant of appropriate boundaries.

Sex and politics are therefore intertwined in many ways. The politically oppressed are often sexually oppressed, while the oppressor consciously or unconsciously uses sex, directly or indirectly, as a weapon to sustain oppression. And both sides understand this at least at some level, as revealed in their language.

3. The economics of oppression is an economics of sexual parallelism: women's work tends to be minorities' work, and vice versa.

Both at the professional and at the less-skilled and unskilled levels, the type of work done by blacks and Latinos (the most obvious examples) is often the type of work done by women, and the type of paid (in the official labor force) work done by women is also characteristic of racial minorities. At the less-skilled and unskilled levels of the growing proportion of low-level manufacturing jobs, for example in high tech (Silicon Valley), food service, and housekeeping (janitorial) jobs, the categories of "women" and "minorities" have now become synonymous. These simply are, in very high proportions, minority women's jobs. Put another way, women take jobs traditionally, that is stereotypically, held by minorities, and minorities take jobs stereotypically called "women's jobs," and minority women take jobs associated with either.

Small wonder that when such work at the lower skill levels is available, the African-American male prefers not to accept it. He has enough problems "getting screwed" in American society without being "womanized" further by the job, apart from the fact that it is low paid. At the lowest levels of employment, the jobs minority people get paid to do are done for free by women in every home: sweeping, washing dishes, cooking, babysitting. That is, these jobs are done for free by those women who cannot afford, or do not wish to hire, minority women to do them. When the white woman is "liberated" to return to a prior professional career, it is usually a minority woman who must replace her in the home, usually part-time. A recent exception is the appearance in paid homemaking of recent women immigrants from Eastern Europe. These are not usually considered "minority," though functionally they are indistinguishable from many other homemakers, especially other immigrants whose command of English is minimal or nil. They just happen, by historical accident, to be white.

At the higher employment levels it continues to be true that many members of minority groups, both men and women, enter fields that are traditionally those of white women. As a number of studies have shown, the distribution of African-American male professionals more closely approximates that of women, both white and black, than that of white men. In general, black women have a better chance of entering professions traditionally associated with women than black men have of entering professions open to men. Indeed, black men have a better chance of entering "women's" professions such as public school teaching and social work than they have of entering "men's" professions such as engineering. This has not changed much in the past several decades, as data showing the small numbers and percentages of African-American males in various professions indicate.

With the continuing decline of union-wage, decently paid manufacturing jobs, black workers can only move up or down. Twenty-five years ago, Manning Marable tells us in *How Capitalism Underdeveloped Black America,* one out of four black workers was employed in manufacturing, which paid midlevel wages. Beginning in the 1980s there was a significant downward shift; by 2000, 26.3 percent of black men and 36.5 percent of black women were in poverty-level jobs. The percentage of Latino men earning poverty-level wages increased from 27.1 percent in 1979 to 37.6 percent in 2000. About half of all Latinas earned poverty-level wages in 2000. Of course many African-Americans continue to work in what remains of the manufacturing sector, but those who lose their jobs and are able to secure new ones find their wages typically lower, the consequence of the type of job that is available: in such "gray collar" areas as food service and janitorial work. William Julius Wilson points out in his analysis of black poverty (*When Work Disappears: The World of the New Urban Poor*) that as the share of young black men in manufacturing fell, it increased dramatically in retail and service jobs, where wages are 25 to 30 percent lower. These are the jobs that are symbolically extensions of household work.

The low prestige of jobs held, typically, by minorities, women, and minority women is generally reinforced by the media. "He-man" jobs in this society are, with the exception of sports, still rarely depicted as held by minorities or women, even though one can nowadays come up with a respectable list of exceptions. On television, the overwhelming majority of detectives, sailors, cattlemen, engineers, sportscar drivers, horse owners, and administrators of large enterprises such as hospitals, movie empires, political parties, or police departments and the like are white men. The notable exception seems to be women newsanchors; however, most of them appear to be chosen at least in part for their looks, especially their blond "American" looks. There are minority women anchors, especially on local stations nowadays, but again, one suspects they appear to be chosen because they approximate Americans' notion of good looks. Older women on camera in any capacity are rare indeed.

The progress of minority men on television can be measured by Bill Cosby, who graduated from being a Tonto to a white spy to an upper bourgeois, totally successful, and utterly "American" (that is, non-ethnic) physician. But Cosby, in any of his roles, was still an exception at the time. In some sitcoms nowadays one sees blacks as police officers or in other stable working-class jobs, and in other shows even in roles as superiors: a high school principal or the occasional police commissioner. But the majority of black males appearing on television are criminals filmed in "documentary" police shows or on the five o'clock local news.

The "traditional" professional jobs held by gay men (at least in myth and fiction—empirical data are quite weak here) are also female, e.g. hairdressing or interior decorating. In lesbian circles, anecdotal evidence also suggests a sexual division of labor: characteristically male jobs (construction) for the "butch," female jobs (secretary) for the "femme." Jobs held by most women, many gays, and (disproportionally) minorities are devalued by society (including, often, by those holding them), even when they are professional (teachers, librarians). Whether they are looked down on because they are seen as "women's work" or whether they are jobs done by women because they are simply available (partly because men shy away from them), or whether, most likely, this constitutes a vicious cycle, is ultimately irrelevant.

As for TV women, most continue to be nurses, social workers, or executive secretaries. Again, there are notable exceptions such as Murphy Brown, but look at the storm she unleashed by being an unmarried mom. In police work women have frequently taken over the Tonto role. They often prove to be so emotional as to be unreliable in a crisis. Those who are cool turn out to be murderers. As for contest shows, watched by tens of millions, the role of women (other than contestants) is often limited to spinning a wheel and the like, and walking about in a short skirt, high heels, and fluffy blond hair.

The media support an image of the labor force that is in part true: demeaning work is for the oppressed, and what the oppressed do is defined as demeaning. The most demeaning work is household-type work, or extensions, in modern technological terms, of household work. And, it should be emphasized, this demeaning definition is supported by wages that are also demeaning. Women's work (especially minority women's work) is the worst paid in this society except for farm labor, some of which is also done by women, especially minority women. Male farm labor and yard work for middle-class and wealthier suburbanites is mostly done by minorities, especially immigrant minorities.

4. The family (the political organization of sexual relations) differs in form for oppressor and oppressed.

In the 1960s, some hippie communes structured their families in ways not much different from the so-called broken, or disfunctional, family so much maligned by the late sociologist and U.S. Senator Daniel Patrick Moynihan and others. Here is a description of one by Gerald Dworkin, writing in *Dissent* magazine in 1969: "the typical . . . household is . . . a heterogeneous grouping of six or eight people, some of them, perhaps, being children, linked to each other by ties which are in many ways family-like. Important decisions are made corporately, possessions are shared, children are cared for by whoever is around and in good condition, sexual partners are not clearly demarcated." This description could apply to any stringently economically-deprived group. It is a political organization of kinship (including sex) structured to cope with a wider type of political oppression, whether involuntary or, as with hippies or other commune-type families such as some utopian communities, voluntary. The striking thing is that the form devised voluntarily is not far removed from the form evolved involuntarily, the so-called disorganized family associated with welfare recipients and other very poor people regardless of race, cross-culturally, cross-historically, and cross-nationally. In point of fact, of course, as the above description suggests, it is not disorganized at all. But it is certainly different from the "normal" American middle-class family, whatever that is nowadays (since fewer than 16 percent of Americans live in a home in which a father is the sole member in the official labor force, the marriage is the first for both partners, and the children are theirs and only theirs).

But there is one difference: the communal family is generally bifocal (centering on both mother and father); the involuntarily oppressed family is often matrifocal (and matriarchal: ruled by mother). The oppressed community seeks to move from matriarchy to patriarchy, which is linked in the minds of many to a decent middle-income existence, while the hippie, who was fed up with suburban patriarchy (actually matriarchy in many ways since Dad was absent most of the time) sought a family of a new kind. Ironically it seems that both the oppressed and the "culturally oppressed" want to move away from a Mom-centered existence, though for quite different reasons.

Family form tends to be congruent with the particular place in the oppressive order that the members of the family occupy. At the top of the stratification system, the oppressor requires a womanservant to run his home (his wife as executive director, with other women, often minorities, under her, and perhaps a man, the gardener/pool guy). The extremely oppressed require a matriarchal, extended family in order to survive, since male breadwinners are in short supply. The less oppressed (the mainstream working class and other middle stratum wage-earners) segment their families in order to work. If one person's income (the man's) is insufficient to maintain a decent standard of living (increasingly the case) the woman must do a double-day. (Younger, childless couples seem to share the housework somewhat more equitably nowadays.)

The relationship of the sexes to each other in the form of the family implies a politics of power (in the form of "archy"). In turn the nature of the "archy" is a response to wider social conditions (of work, income, and cultural practice). This of course affects the internal dynamics of the family, including, presumably, its sexual dynamics, its socialization patterns, and its role modeling, each of which correspondingly differs from family type to family type. All of this boils down to saying that the political organization of sexual relations is class linked and given that fact, to speak of a "normal" or "typical" American family type, "normal" sexual dynamics or "normal" socialization patterns, is quite impossible given that such an average type cannot exist in a class-divided and racist society.

5. Reactions to rejection on sexual grounds parallel reactions to rejection on sociopolitical grounds.

It is only logical that if sex and politics are so closely linked in society, then the victim's reaction to rejection, exclusion, or discrimination on sexual grounds will be similar in form to his/her reaction to rejection on other grounds, and vice versa. Gordon Allport noted a long time ago that many minority groups try, at least at first, to gain acceptance into the dominant society. Indeed, the media generally advertise "integration" (amalgamation?), including the elimination of "undesirable" foreign (non "middle-class"), traits as the path to follow for individual minority group members. But there are three levels of "acceptance:" one level, which leaves social relations undisturbed, forces the minority person to play a role supportive of existing steriotypes. This is hardly integration. Rather, it is the maintenance of a false stability based on oppression. Thus the phenomenon of the Uncle Tom, the Uncle Jake, the Aunt Jane, the Uncle Tomahawk, are all means of adapting, or of being "accepted" at a certain level in order to assure personal survival within the system. This is what many women continue to do; after all, it is the way they, and the men in their lives, have been socialized.

Another level implies acceptance into the present order on an equal basis with those who now run it, that is, becoming amalgamated. This often includes internalizing the norms, including negative stereotypes about minorities, of the dominant group. Hence the oreo cookie, the apple (red on the outside, white on the inside), and other terms are ways of adapting and being accepted at the price of surrendering all vestiges of one's previous groupness. The corporate woman, attache case in hand, fully dressed in a slightly feminized version of the male pinstripe, symbolizes this approach.

The third level, that of being accepted on the basis of one's authentic self and group identity, is something else again. It is not really acceptance (a one-way process) but reciprocity. It may not mean integration at all.

Acceptance of a sexual minority, as in the case of gays or women (who, although a majority, constitute a "sociological minority"), seems to be at least as difficult for straight men as acceptance of other minorities, even though on the surface it might appear that fewer vested interests are involved. After all, if African-Americans vote in the South, this implies profound challenges to the political and economic status quo. How is property challenged by homosexuals? Yet at another level, almost needless to say, the challenge to the straight, powerful, or macho sexual self-image posed, apparently, by gays, or by liberated women, appears to be quite threatening to other forms of vested interest, including the sacred bourgeois family. Underneath all the talk about "family values," then, is a profound fear that the independent woman is a destructive force, destructive primarily of male economic domination within the family, but also subversive of the "traditional" family unit itself. And this does challenge the system, for the family unit (insofar as it still exists) is the institution that is responsible for the reproduction of the labor force. Insofar as it decays, the stability of Capital itself is threatened.

It is easy enough for men to accept women at the first level, that of women playing the role assigned them by society. The playing of the sub-servient role calls forth a safe, paternalistic reaction. But this is acceptance based on a continuation of oppression. The second type of acceptance is that form so long sought after by many, though not all, suffragists and their heirs: that of full integration into the men's world of today, that is, subordinating one's feminine qualities to the needs of the masculine organizational world, and claiming full equality to men in every respect within the present system. Many political forces in both women's organizations and homophile groups (as well as most conventional civil rights organizations) share this approach. Note, for example, the long effort by gay lobbies to get homosexuals into the armed forces and obtain for them equal rights in that institution. This strat-egy requires strenuous efforts to convince the public of gays' unquestioning loyalty and patriotism.

The third type of acceptance, if that is what it is (perhaps *autonomy* or *authenticity* would be better terms) was increasingly sought by the social move-ments of the late '60s and '70s. Black Power, gay liberation, women's liberation were all symptomatic of this third response to rejection. Women began to re-ject both sexual popularity at the price of authenticity, and the surrender of sexuality in order to become corporate movers and shakers. Equality without exploitation but also without an equally inauthentic mannishness was increas-ingly seen as desirable by many in the women's movement. Later, some men began to grapple with what they had come to see as a fraudulent macho im-age. This struggle continues today and constitutes a component of the current "men's group movement."

However, both the second and third types of acceptance are difficult to achieve because both involve challenges to certain vested interests, especially in the labor market. And so, continued rejection must be coped with. The vari-ous psychological coping mechanisms used by individuals in dealing with re-jection were catalogued by Gordon Allport long ago. In the end, they prove inadequate, and rejection (that is, being victimized by discriminatory treatment of one kind or another, direct or indirect, conscious or unconscious) must be dealt with not on an individual but on a group level. These mechanisms, both individual and group, are discussed in detail in chapter 7.

In this chapter five propositions in which sex and politics are related have been described: 1) that the extreme of oppression is sexual use and abuse; 2) that political positions are often seen in sexual terms and vice versa; 3) that women's work is minorities' work and vice versa; 4) that oppressed groups' or-ganization of sexual relations (family structure) is different from oppressor groups' organization; and 5) that people react to being rejected on sexual grounds in much the same way they react to other kinds of group rejection.

None of these propositions is much more than common sense, based on everyday observation. Yet taken together one cannot help but conclude that the sexual dimension of social life is a profoundly political fact; and conversely, that the political dimension of social life (that is, the dimension of subordination and superordination, of power) can scarcely be comprehended without attention to sexuality and the way it is socially organized.

• 4 •

Dealing with Minorities:
From Genocide to Integration[1]

$\mathcal{R}$ichard Jordan Gatling and Hiram Maxim, two Americans, invented the forerunners of the contemporary heavy machine gun in 1862 and 1884, respectively. These early versions of the machine gun were "a vital useful tool in the colonisation of Africa," military historian John Ellis tells us in his illuminating *The Social History of the Machine Gun*. On August 14, 1904 the Herero people began an uprising against their German colonial rulers in what was then German Southwest Africa (now Namibia). 65,000 Herero and 10,000 Nama tribesmen were massacred, mostly by machine gun fire, in what has been called the first genocide of the twentieth century. The United Nations, following World War II, defined genocide as "the denial of the right of existence of entire human groups," in other words the deliberate attempt to physically destroy a population deemed undesirable or superfluous for whatever reason. Although hardly unique to the twentieth century, genocide became its defining tragedy.

Genocide is one "agenda" that the modern state has used to maintain the supremacy of one particular group over another. All states have agendas, formal or informal, regarding their minority groups because they must deal somehow with the fact that minorities are always disadvantaged relative to the dominant ethnic group (except of course where a minority, for example white Anglo-Saxon Episcopalians, *is* the dominant group). As a result, these disadvantaged groups constitute a threat to the existing order. We have already seen that minorities bear the brunt of victimization by hate, bigotry, stereotyping, and abuse by individuals; now we need to look at how governments create environments that encourage, promote, and execute (in several senses of the term)

---

1. Sections of this chapter are drawn from chapter 7 of the author's *The State in Modern Society* (Humanity Books, 2000).

policies about the minorities that live under their jurisdictions—or, conversely, how they discourage the persecution of minorities, promoting rather policies that lead to equal treatment. It is unfortunately the case that the dominant ethnicity perpetually resists equalization or integration in varying degrees because the integration of minorities in the economy, in the political structure, and in "society" or the aristocracy cannot be accommodated without profound alterations in the economic structure, in political institutions, and in elite social institutions. Each of these involves vested interests that can at best only partially accommodate the demands, and the large-scale personal participation, of subordinate ethnic groups.

The economic or class structure in its concrete, daily form translates into the workings of the labor market and the occupational system. The Herero case is an extreme: the Europeans sought to exclude the Herero entirely from participation in their colonial society. Not only the Germans in Southwest Africa, but all of the European colonial powers, and not only in Africa but also in other parts of the colonial and postcolonial world, engaged in what is today called "ethnic cleansing," the physical elimination, by wholesale murder or by forced expulsion, of some ethnic minority by the dominant group. The United States in its policy toward various Native-American nations was no exception. Even slavery is not so extreme.

But even when a subordinate minority has the same access to the set of occupations in the labor market as the dominant group, which to an extent is true in most modern capitalist societies, they do not share equal incomes and equal positions of power. Generally minorities have an occupational distribution that is inferior, as measured by the income, wealth, and power that various occupations generate. The subordinate group seeks to maintain its ethnic identity as a form of mutual support in a discriminatory environment, but the dominant group also seeks to maintain ethnic labeling as an exclusionary mechanism in order to maintain its advantages. Discrimination based on ethnicity (including race, religion, language, immigrant status, or some combination of these) has the function of maintaining control by the dominant social class, which is also the dominant (though often not the majority) ethnic group. To one extent or another the state reinforces this inequity, whether by deliberate, legal policies of discrimination and segregation (as in the old South or the old South Africa or in the early years of Hitler's Germany), or merely by benign neglect (the policy of doing nothing to compensate for minority disadvantages rooted in past practices).

Conflicts over resources in an ethnically homogeneous society (Norway or Denmark, perhaps, a hundred years ago) are simple: it is the owning class versus the others, straightforward class conflict. But no such society exists today. Conflicts over resources are therefore much more complex because they intersect class stratification with ethnic stratification. Since it is the job of the state to assure stability for whatever class structure exists, it must develop an agenda to cope with minorities. But states differ in their agendas because the way class intersects with minorities differs from place to place and time to time. States confront challenges to their stability and legitimacy from a number of sources, not only the potential of minority protest and uprising, and they must develop a project to deal with these challenges. These challenges range from immediate economic crisis often accompanied by the rise of radical mass movements, to nation-building (creating a unified nation out of disparate ethnicities), overcoming backward economic relationships, creating a supply of labor adequate to a developing economy, and of course defending the nation against outside threats.

Many of these projects interact with one another, and have led to, or reinforced, the scapegoating of some minority, with discrimination and quasi-castelike separation between different groups, and the exclusion of minorities from certain occupations, housing, education, and political representation. The debates about these agendas for dealing with minorities are expressed in a variety of ideological terms, ranging from the crudest racism all the way to support for civil rights in a society that requires a relatively rational exploitation of human resources and a minimization of conflict. These debates are mirrored by debates within the minority community as to the causes of, and solutions to, their "problem."

What are the different agendas that states have used to "deal" with their minorities? At one extreme there is the fascist or Nazi state, which comes to power in a period of acute economic crisis. Mass movements of a fascist type promote a "solution" to this crisis by scapegoating one or more minorities and mobilizing the nation for war. Since mobilization requires national unity and minorities potentially stand in the way, they become de facto enemy aliens and, together with political dissidents, are doomed to imprisonment and sometimes physical extinction. For the Nazis racism and specifically anti-Semitism were part of the program from the start. The demonization and dehumanization of an enemy is not unique to fascism, but it is significantly more pronounced because there are no forces within the country that might call for a moderation of such extreme measures. They have all been frightened off, or themselves imprisoned. The Nazi "final solution," according to R. J. Rummel in *Death By Government,* "likely cost the lives of about 16,300,000 people: nearly 5,300,000 Jews, 260,000 Gypsies, 10,500,000 Slavs, and 220,000 homosexuals as well as another 170,000 handicapped Germans."

The authoritarian states that are still all too common in the Third World present a more varied picture. The fundamental problem is that many now independent states were once colonies whose borders were drawn by the European powers, and redrawn after wars, without regard to existing ethnic differences. The agenda of the newly independent rulers, in their drive to modernize, requires what is called "nation-building." There are existing ethnic subgroups that differ in religion, language, and history from those of the ruling group. With independence, they now seek the autonomy that was denied them by their former colonial masters in this irreverent drawing of political borders. But this implies a splintering of the new nation that cannot be tolerated by the nation-building project. Hence attempts at their suppression lead to long-term conflicts including bloody civil wars, as in several African countries.

A different problem with many of the same consequences resulted from the breakup of ancient empires that had always been multiethnic. These sprawling feudal powers, such as the Ottoman, Russian, and Austro-Hungarian empires, collapsed after World War I. Austria-Hungary was imperfectly carved up into a set of nations, each of which contained very large minorities with their own national identities. The Ottoman Empire was divided into one semi-modern nation (Turkey) and numerous colonies under the domination of the victors of World War I, again with little regard for how this might have divided existing ethnic entities. In all probability only the 1917 Russian revolution prevented the complete disintegration of the Czarist Empire, a centrifugal process that resumed with the collapse of the Soviet Union in the 1990s.

This is not to say that the former large multiethnic states or colonies (like India) were societies of peaceful coexistence, since even in those days minority ethnicities occupied subordinate positions and consequently organized movements for autonomy, or even total independence. But they were at least nominally tolerated and given some local autonomy. Once the overall structure collapsed or was abandoned (as in many colonies), minority ethnic groups felt they had a license to strike out for independence. The agenda of modernization and nation-building ran counter to the rhetoric of self-determination, and the new governments sometimes took extreme measures to guarantee national unity.

Excluding mass murders in various colonies and the United States by modern armies and settlers, the first truly organized genocide of the twentieth century was the virtual elimination of the Armenians by Turkey. Nearly two million Armenians were killed between 1915 and 1923, including most of the 200,000 or so Armenians who had been drafted into the Turkish army. The nationalist spirit of the "Young Turks," who were bent on creating a unified modern state uncluttered by minorities, was part of the equation. Turkey today continues to be plagued by internal unrest, mainly in Kurdish regions. Since 1992 between 2.5 and 5 million Kurds have been forcibly expelled from their homelands and scattered into cities as part of a long-term strategy of what amounts to "ethnocide," the deliberate attempt to destroy an entire culture without necessarily exterminating its people. Recently, however, as part of its campaign to enter the European Union, Turkey has made moves to be more tolerant of Kurdish culture.

In many developing nations today the issue is not nation-building with the associated need to eliminate "troublesome" minority nationalities. Instead, it is the need to sustain minorities (mainly the aboriginal population) as a source of cheap labor to work on plantations, in mines, and otherwise to supply low-cost labor. Their participation at the lower levels of the global economy is essential, not only as household servants for the local middle and upper classes, but more importantly as workers in the sweatshop or "maquiladora" system.[2] As agribusiness comes to dominate agriculture and bankrupt peasants, who are either aboriginals or "mixed" race, they are driven to the urban areas and into maquiladora work if it is available. If not, the alternatives are prostitution for women, crime for men, peddling, or migrating to "First World" countries, legally or not.

The colonial period was characterized by the large-scale destruction of native populations by gunfire, disease, starvation, and the ravages of forced labor. But in Latin America even after independence from Spain, suffrage was so restricted that "Indians" were effectively barred from the political process. Many millions of indigenous people found themselves outcasts, remaining in their traditional tribal areas. They escaped the fate of living in urban slums only to find themselves surviving at a below-subsistence level in jungle or hill areas, always subject to the whim of the government, often in the form of the local military. The explosion of the Zapatista Army of National Liberation in Chiapas, Mexico, in 1994 was a graphic demonstration of the continued suffering, and resistance, of poor peasants throughout all of Central and South America, who are disproportionally of indigenous background. The Zapatistas of today are concentrated in Mayan regions and speak at least four different native languages.

Aboriginals constitute the absolute poorest populations in the world today. Whether driven off their lands or remaining there to scratch out a miserable existence on marginal lands or in government-sponsored reservations (sometimes as tourist curiosities), whether lucky enough to find low-level employment as household servants or unfortunate enough to find themselves on the streets begging, they are easily identifiable (by their clothing and color), stigmatized, discriminated against, and when they mobilize to change their condition, brutally repressed by armed force. But it does well to remember that

---

2. A maquiladora is generally understood to be a subcontracting factory where components are assembled by low-skilled, often women workers, to be shipped to the contracting corporation in another country, often with low or no duties levied. Typically, the product is garments or electronic devices such as cell phones. The author's cell phone was assembled in a maquiladora in Tijuana, Mexico.

these populations, no matter how poor, are not redundant. Their very stigmatization forces them into necessary sectors of the economy, especially those associated with "dirty work" (dishwashers, gardeners, maids, and of course low-level factory labor). Their low wages also act as a deterrent to other workers' asking for more. And their lowly status enables workers just above them to feel superior.

Outright extermination is no longer an acceptable policy for modern states, even when their histories have often exhibited genocidal moments with respect to native populations, and even though they may tolerate it in other states, dallying while large numbers of people are massacred and debating whether or not to call it genocide. Moreover, these minorities are needed to play certain roles in the economy. But the pattern of the old empires, where minorities had some minimal cultural and political autonomy, is equally unacceptable except perhaps in Canada, and secession has really not been permitted by any modern state. Anyway it is impractical. How would such a group, lacking significant capital, technical skills, and (frequently) access to raw materials, survive in a global economy? Neither outright repression nor independent existence is consistent with the economic project of modern capitalism, which requires that political units be unified and that employers have access to a wide range of labor power that is organized in a rational way. Moreover, a modern economy requires social peace, a prerequisite for a positive investment climate, so that somehow minorities must be accommodated.

The range of opinions and debates concerning the degree to which minorities are to be integrated within modern societies, and how this is to take place, is quite extensive. These debates fluctuate over time between acceptance of minorities (and immigrants) and hostility (and exclusionary policies). The need for particular kinds of labor is a powerful determinant of governmental strategy, especially rules about immigration and citizenship. But politics also plays an important role. Powerful political forces scapegoat immigrants, blaming them for unemployment just as they scapegoat welfare recipients for causing allegedly high taxes. U.S. immigration policy, as well as immigration policy in a number of other Western countries and even Japan, is therefore caught in a tug of war between employers' need for labor at both unskilled and certain skilled levels, and some workers' (and their unions') perception that immigrants threaten their jobs. Playing into the latter, especially when unemployment for the local unskilled is high, is the xenophobic notion that immigrants are a threat to some set of "American" or "German" or "Corsican" and/or "Christian" (especially when it comes to Muslim immigrants) values. In Corsica, a formerly fairly homogeneous population, about ten percent of the 260,000 inhabitants consists of Moroccan Arabs, who were brought there for agricultural work. Locals, fearing that their Christian culture is under attack, have responded with a campaign of bombing houses of worship and business establishments in order to encourage the exit of the Muslims. In Germany, particularly in the east where unemployment is very high, neo-Nazi skinheads regularly rampage about, attacking and even murdering dark-skinned immigrants.

The definition of a citizen varies from country to country and different historical traditions become political weapons in the service of one or another agenda, but almost inevitably, whatever the tradition, the immigrant ends up in a subordinate position compared to the "native." There are states (Germany, and, paradoxically, Israel) that base citizenship on membership in the ethnicity, the "Volk," on the "law of blood," so that there is a legal right of return for those who belong although their families may not have lived in that respective country for centuries and they may not even speak the language. This can then become the rationale for excluding others when their usefulness to the labor force has been exhausted. Turks who came to Germany in a period of labor shortages after World War II cannot readily become German citizens no matter how long they have lived there; even their children are not automatically citizens.

Other countries, such as France, are committed to a form of secularism in which to be a citizen means to be totally integrated. The assumption is that there are universal norms common to the definition of being French that everyone should adhere to. This implies censure and even persecution of ethnicities such as Arab Muslims when they become inconvenient with respect to the labor market. The law does not permit young Arab women to wear headscarves in public schools. Many Germans and French, not to mention the citizens of numerous other countries with significant immigrant populations, share the fear that immigrants, especially those with dark skins and different religions, will undermine or dilute their respective cultures.

The United States and Canada, as nations founded by settlers, both contain very large minorities. Canada contains an entire province, Quebec, which differs markedly from the rest of the nation in language, religion, and historical consciousness. A very active movement for Quebec independence has been in existence for a long time, and although independence is unlikely, the price for domestic peace is that Canada has had to work out some special provisions to give Quebec greater autonomy on a number of issues. Complicating the matter further is the existence (in both Canada and the United States) of large "First Nation" or "Native American" nations. The United States also contains within its political boundaries a quasi-colony, Puerto Rico (plus a few other smaller island possessions). But beyond that, the United States is host to two very large "racial" minorities, African-Americans and Mexican-Americans (by far the largest Spanish-speaking group). Both Canada and the United States continue to debate policy toward minorities. Both straddle the fence between integration (the melting pot idea) and cultural pluralism (the patchwork quilt notion), with Canada leaning more to the latter. These debates are increasing in countries such as Spain and Italy, where fifty years ago immigration was a distinctly minor issue. But there has been an influx of both legal and illegal immigrants seeking better economic opportunities in more recent years.

But whatever the situation, the minority group, immigrant or native, suffers disadvantages in accessing resources, and is the victim of economic and political exploitation. Even well-educated and technically-trained immigrants coming to the United States to seek work or brought here by corporations to fill job vacancies suffer some forms of discrimination, especially when they are dark-skinned.

Debates about how to "solve" the minority "question" go back more than a century in social scientific theorizing and research; in turn, social science thinking has influenced the wider debate, and has affected public policy for both good and bad. Racist theories about the inherent inferiority of certain groups do persist and make comebacks, as we saw in the previous chapter. Their persistence poses political dangers in the form of anti-immigrant and anti-Semitic tendencies within even some major political parties, not to mention independent parties focusing on these issues, in countries as widely separated as Denmark, France, Germany, Austria, and of course the heartlands of traditional anti-Semitism, the countries east of the German-Polish border. Blatantly racist ideas, however, have been generally discredited and are no longer a dominant part of public discourse even though many individuals continue to hold them.

A more common view is that the presence of large numbers of immigrants, ethnic minorities, and indeed the entire project called cultural pluralism (or multiculturalism) endangers national cohesiveness, leads to conflict, and more generally threatens to undermine "Western civilization," or "Judeo-Christian values." The "English Only" movement in the United States, which is aimed at the multiculturalism represented by multilingual education, or having government documents available in Spanish and other languages, is an example of this view.

In the United States this was a minor chord until September 11, 2001. Since that time anti-immigrant sentiment has been growing. The U.S. government in the form of the Department of Immigration and Customs Enforcement (DICE) has conducted "roundups" of undocumented aliens (some from the countries of the Middle East and Southern Asia but most of them from Mexico and Central America), and has deported an unknown number. In response, an immigrant rights movement has sprung up. (It is entirely reasonable to anticipate that immigration will be the next civil rights issue in the United States, as it already is in a number of European countries.)

The most common view about minorities in social scientific circles is what Michael Omi and Howard Winant, in their very important book *Racial Formation in the United States,* call the "ethnicity paradigm." This model proceeds on two assumptions: first, that all minority groups are ethnic in nature and face basically similar problems, and second, that given appropriate social policies (particularly opening educational and occupational opportunities) all groups will eventually replicate the history of previous groups and become fitted for citizenship. It follows that if a group continues to be disadvantaged, it is either because opportunities are still blocked, the case for legislation, or that there is something wrong with their method of adjustment, the case for blaming their maladaptive culture. The former approach is that of classical reform liberalism; the latter is useful for scapegoating and fits into right-wing populist demagogy.

The famous group of sociologists at the University of Chicago called "The Chicago School" proposed, in a series of studies back in the 1920s and 1930s, that there was a process in which immigrant and other minority groups would inevitably assimilate. Even racially different groups would follow this road. As the founder of the "School," Robert E. Park, put it, "Racial barriers may slacken the tempo of the movement; may perhaps halt it altogether for a time, but cannot change its direction; cannot, at any rate reverse it . . . the forces which have brought about the existing interpenetration of peoples are so vast and irresistible that the resulting changes assume the character of a cosmic process."

This perspective was adopted, with minor modifications, by Swedish social scientist Gunnar Myrdal many years later in his famous study of race relations, *An American Dilemma* (1944). He saw the "Negro Problem" primarily as a moral one, pitting the American creed of equality against the realities of discrimination, and concluded that enlightened elites would lead the nation to improve its institutions and overcome this discrepancy between values and realities. Myrdal held that modern capitalism itself held the clue to the solution: prejudice and discrimination were incompatible with a modern, rational economy. As the South modernized, racism would diminish.

The shortcoming of this theory, as Omi and Winant make clear, is that different groups have quite different histories, bringing different kinds of capital with them (economic capital, human capital or education, and social capital, or connections, networks, and the know-how about social interaction that is so helpful in getting ahead). They differ in numbers and timing (how many people? How many and what kinds of jobs are available?). And minorities identifiable as racially different have a tougher time given the legacy of racism that exists in virtually all "democracies." In short, the playing field is not level. What liberal theorists believe is that the playing field can be made level through reform legislation.

It would be foolish to say that African-Americans have made no progress since Park wrote in the 1920s, or Myrdal following World War II. The terror of the Klan in the South has been virtually eliminated, and African-Americans play increasing roles at all levels of the political process. In addition, more and more have attained college educations, and have entered the middle and up-per-middle strata of the economy. Nevertheless, without belaboring the point here, very large proportions of the African-American population continue to suffer disadvantages. From poverty and unemployment rates to infant mortal-ity, from educational facilities to treatment by the criminal justice system, from access to affordable housing to even the traditional problem of the right to suffrage, African-Americans (and, nowadays, Latinos as well) are often disad-vantaged.

If such conditions are incompatible, or dysfunctional, with modern capi-talism (because they prevent the economy from fully utilizing labor, increase the costs of welfare and related measures, limit incomes and consumption, and promote social conflict), why has Park's prophecy not been more fully fulfilled? An alterative set of theories that emphasize institutional constraints may pro-vide some help. This theory begins with the classical Marxian axiom that is the reverse of Myrdal's: racism *is* functional to capitalism; indeed capitalism could not exist without it. The classical view is that the capitalist class utilizes racism as an instrument to keep the working class divided, hence prevents the unity that is necessary to progress. As Oliver Cromwell Cox, an African-American sociologist, wrote in a typical statement back in 1948, "Today it is of vital con-sequence that black labor and white labor in the South be kept glaring at each other, for if they were permitted to come together in force and to identify their interests as workers, the difficulty of exploiting them would be increased be-yond calculation." Capitalist entrepreneurs have played the "race card" on in-numerable occasions to undermine unionization campaigns, scapegoat African-Americans and other minorities, including immigrants, for economic troubles, and convince white workers to vote for conservative politicians and against their clear economic interests as workers.

But there is more: inasmuch as discrimination functions to exclude peo-ple from some kinds of jobs, it provides the mechanism to locate those people in the lower-paid and less-skilled strata of the labor market that are necessary for the operation of the system; and, by maintaining unequal educational and job opportunities, to guarantee an army of the un- and underemployed to act as a drag on the wages and working conditions of the employed. A labor force that, over history, comes to lock different groups into some occupations, and lock them out of others, assures their availability at a given wage. No occupa-tion contains within it a random selection of the population. No group (eth-nic, racial, or gender) is randomly distributed throughout the labor force. All of these factors combine to guarantee the survival, and profitability, of the present economic system. But it does not explain the terrible unemployment, crime, and welfare rates of some inner city areas. Their costs in welfare, policing, disease, and mortality undoubtedly exceed the benefits of political scapegoating or having people available to work in the fast-food industry. The only clear benefit is to the prison industry, the immense cost of which is hardly helpful to the taxpayers.

Sociologist William Julius Wilson, in a series of books such as *When Work Disappears* (1996), explains that economic forces that have little to do with racism as such have a disproportionally negative impact on African-American communities. Even as blacks migrated to the big cities from the post-slavery South these cities were beginning to lose their industrial base. The hard core of the black working class became concentrated in the very industries that were soon to move to the non-union South and offshore (Detroit's auto industry is the prime example). The growth sectors in employment required educational levels not widely available in the ghetto, or were located outside the cities. The consequences are devastating: "High rates of joblessness trigger other neighborhood problems that undermine social organization, ranging from crime, gang violence, and drug trafficking to family breakup and problems in the organization of family life."

Between 1970 and 2002, 27 of the largest 100 cities in the United States lost population; at least 20 of those have significant numbers of African-Americans and in many cases their numbers increased while the numbers of whites (and middle-class blacks) decreased. All of them are in the East or Midwest, many in the so-called rust belt of the industrial heartland. As union-level, decently paid jobs leave, the tax income of cities declines, and the cities' infractructures, especially public education, begin to deteriorate. High school graduation rates decline and large numbers of minority teenagers lack the educational levels required of the new economy of computers, even assuming jobs of that kind existed in the cities (mainly they are in the suburbs). Seeing the gradual decay of public education, families who are able to do so abandon the public school system. Many move out. The cycle of deterioration continues, and the conditions described by Wilson worsen.

How does the state, in the form of public policy, deal with this crisis? One gimmick after another is tried, as public officials seek a "magic bullet" way out. In education, charter schools and innovative small public schools work for a few students, but not for thousands of others. Increased policing helps stabilize the environment so that people can get to work and back safely. But most jobs that serve downtown businesses are in the low-paid sectors (fast food or hotel work) and those in the suburbs are similarly dead-end (housekeeping or gardening). Casinos or other tourist attractions such as Camden, New Jersey's aquarium or Trenton, New Jersey's sports stadiums generate jobs, but most of them, too, are low-paid. In any case there are not enough of them to put much of a dent in the unemployment figures. Trenton lost one-third of its manufacturing jobs between 1990 and 2000. It has twice the state's unemployment rate. One-fourth of the adult population lacks a high school degree. One out of five Trentonians lives under the official poverty line. If Trenton were not the state capital, its equivalent, as one observer said, of Atlantic City's casinos, and did not have numerous health care facilities to provide work, conditions would be even worse.

The fact is there is no magic bullet. Better educational facilities (smaller classes, more computers), more crime control, increased drug counseling, creating waterfront parks, having Habitat for Humanity build twenty units of housing, restoring historical districts, and attracting handfuls of young professionals to return to the city—all these and many other schemes are useful but will not, even in combination, turn these cities around and create decent living conditions for the large mass of their inhabitants, regardless of ethnicity or race. The single factor that would, large numbers of living-wage jobs, is a factor that is beyond the control of any city. The labor market is driven by global economic forces. Only the federal government has a chance to affect those forces.

Although discrimination is functional to the way some parts of the economy works, it is also dysfunctional to other parts. Discrimination is still quite prevalent in employment, housing, policing, and in the many ways in which people relate to each other at the individual level. It is accompanied by prejudice and bigotry, and sometimes takes the form of hate and hate crimes. But even if these were all completely eliminated by some miracle, the economic conditions that to some degree were historically rooted in discrimination now have a life of their own. The very large minority groups that live in cities are not being assimilated as Park anticipated. If Park meant that barriers to full equality would come down, they have not done so.

It has been argued, for example by Mike Davis in *Magical Urbanism: Latinos Reinvent the U.S. City*, that Latinos, who now outnumber African-Americans in seven of the ten largest cities in the United States, have fundamentally altered the traditional black-white dichotomy in our urban areas, and in a positive way that may change the negative prognosis often associated with the black-dominated rust belt ghettos. "Latinos are bringing redemptive energies to the neglected, worn-out cores and inner suburbs of many metropolitan areas," he writes. In the poorest sections of Los Angeles, "there is not a street that has not been dramatically brightened by new immigrants." Although it is clear that city populations, even in rust belt areas, would be declining even faster without Latino immigration, there is little hard data to support the view that

Latinos will be able to turn most cities around without considerable help from larger economic forces. "Although tens of thousands of Spanish-surnamed businesses testify to a huge pool of entrepreneurial energy, the capitalization of Latino enterprises [in Los Angeles] is generally miniscule," Davis reports, and most Latinos remain concentrated in the lower-paid services and manufacturing sectors. Half the Puerto Ricans in the continental United States are poor. In 2002, 22.7 percent of African Americans and 21.8 percent of Latinos lived below the poverty line.

Mexican day laborers from coast to coast are regularly assaulted by whites. There is constant hysteria in Southern California particularly about the "brown peril" to American institutions. After September 11, 2001, immigrant roundups (mainly targeting Central Americans) became almost routine despite protests from civil liberties and immigrant legal defense organizations. On the other hand there has been a significant upsurge in Latino political representation. Few major non-Hispanic political candidates fail to utter at least a few phrases in Spanish. The political clout, especially of the Mexican-American population, is now widely recognized. And, perhaps more important, labor militancy by Latino service workers has arguably become the key to any chance the U.S. labor movement has of recovering its own political influence.

Despite limited successes, and significant improvement over time for segments of the minority population, the overall picture of life for the majority of the members of the large African-American and Latino minorities is not a happy one. Nor is this limited to the United States. As Howard Winant reminds us in his wide-ranging study *The World Is a Ghetto*, "For the truth is . . . racism survives. . . . Racism still distributes advantages and privileges effectively (at least from the standpoint of the privileged); it still pervades the exercise of political power; it still shapes ideas about history, society, community and identity. . . . Pick any relevant sociological indicator—life expectancy, infant mortality, literacy, access to health care, income levels—and apply it in virtually any setting, global, regional, or local, and the results will be the same: the worldwide correlation of wealth and well-being with white skin and European descent, and of poverty and immiseration with dark skin and 'otherness.'"

What are minorities to do? Is it their lot to permanently remain one-down in our society, with perhaps the exception of some recent immigrant minorities from Asia and the Indian subcontinent? In the final chapter of this book some strategies employed by minorities to overcome their subordinate condition will be explored in detail.

Yes, Virginia, There Are Conspiracies and Sometimes They're Out to Get You

On February 13, 1999, a young Algerian refugee living in a camp for asylum applicants in a small eastern German town died after a group of neo-Nazi skinheads chased him and some buddies out of a bar and he crashed through a glass door in an effort to get away. He severed an artery and bled to death. An incident of this kind takes place somewhere in Germany about every three days, though usually not with such fatal consequences.

On August 9, 2004, five men were indicted in the beating of a Sikh in Queens, New York. They were charged with second-degree assault as a hate crime, and other assault-related crimes. The victim was a fifty-four-year-old limousine driver, who was punched and kicked unconscious and sustained multiple fractures, according to The New York Times. If convicted, the assailants would face up to fifteen years in prison.

Are these two incidents related? Yes and no. In many incidents such as the first one the assailants are young, are likely to lack skills and be unemployed, are school dropouts, come from problem-ridden families characterized by alcoholism, and probably had been on a beer-drinking spree. The assailants in the Sikh case were not skinheads. They ranged in age from twenty-two to fifty-eight and lived in solid middle-income neighborhoods. Three were members of the same family, including two brothers and their stepfather. The skinheads could easily have committed this assault, however; it fit into their normal, everyday activities. What these men all have in common is one thing: hatred of at least one minority. But the skinheads are part of a larger, organized regional and possibly even national movement, even though they were acting spontaneously. The men from Queens were not part of an organized group. But they may be recruitable to a larger enterprise, and in other instances it is clear that "hate crimes" have been influenced, instigated, or directly organized by extreme right-wing organizations.

The April 19, 1995 bombing of a U.S. federal government building in Oklahoma City focused national attention on extremism of the right for the first time in many years. (This incident falls into the definition of "terrorism." More on that in the next chapter.) It put the spotlight in particular on the "militia movement," with which Timothy McVeigh and Terry Nichols, the two convicted bombers, had had some contact. Yet the news that the perpetrators had associations with extreme right-wing groups should hardly have been a surprise. A number of private watchdog organizations had been trying for years to publicize the growing menace of right-wing extremism. The *Turner Diaries*, a kind of right-wing bible, had been available and known to watchdog organizations since 1978. A long series of incidents of right-wing violence had already taken place: Alan Berg, a Jewish radio commentator, had been murdered by members of a group called "The Order" in 1984 (two men were convicted and imprisoned). Jack Oliphant, a member of the "Arizona Patriots," was convicted of planning a robbery, the proceeds of which were to finance his organization, in 1987. He died in prison. Also in 1987, thirteen white supremacists were charged in Fort Smith, Arkansas, with conspiring to overthrow the government. One of the defendants had already spent eight years in prison for bombing school buses. (The Fort Smith defendants were acquitted.) A civil rights group that had been monitoring Ku Klux Klan activities for many years, the Southern Poverty Law Center's Klanwatch, had published the fourth edition of its report, including material on militia training, in 1991. Another watchdog organization, the Anti-Defamation League of B'nai B'rith, a mainstream Jewish organization, had also published reports of "the militia menace." By 1995 a number of books as well as many journalistic reports (mostly in liberal or left publications such as *The Nation*, but not in the mainstream press) were available.

In 1995, so the ADL and the SPLC reported, militias (paramilitary formations with an extremist right-wing political agenda) were operating in all fifty states, with between 20,000 and 50,000 active participants. The SPLC had accumulated files including 11,000 photographs, and reports on some 14,000 individuals and 3,200 right-wing extremist organizations (some of which, it should be mentioned, existed only on paper, or only very briefly). There were at the time probably around 150,000 close sympathizers of a variety of groups associated with the extreme right, including the Ku Klux Klan, neo-Nazi skinheads, Nazis, and what is loosely termed the "Christian Patriot Movement" (some of which overlap with the militias). Both the ADL and the SPLC made its reports available to police at all levels of government. Cross-border links between some U.S. right-wing extremists or "neo-Nazis" and some European groups had also been known for some time, and reported.

Who are these people? What was their relationship to more mainstream U.S. politics, especially the fundamentalist Christian wing of the Republican Party? What sort of threat do these groups actually constitute today?

That some sectors of the ultraright are Nazi is hard to miss. A (Jewish) Professor at the Harvard School of Public Health, Raphael S. Ezekiel, had the "chutzpah" to actually attend a congress of the Aryan Nations group in 1988 (it is reported in his book *The Racist Mind*, published in 1995). There the "Horst Wessel" anthem of the German Nazi Party of Hitler days was played constantly, the Nazi salute was used, the swastika flag was flown, a wreath to Rudolf Hess stood beside a huge sword with a swastika, yet none of these men (it was a male gathering) are Germans or even disproportionately of German descent. The founder of Aryan Nations was a pastor who was also the organizer of its religious wing, the extremely anti-Semitic "Church of Jesus Christ, Christian." Or consider the founder of an organization called White Aryan Resistance (WAR), Tom Metzger. Professor Ezekiel interviewed him several times in the 1980s. His organization, based in Portland, Oregon, was at that time attempting to recruit skinheads, and training them in tactics of street fighting. In 1990 he was ordered to pay $12.5 million to the family of an Ethiopian college student who had been killed by three skinheads incited or trained by WAR. In the Ezekiel interview Metzger talks about a "third force" opposed to both monopoly capitalism and communism. "He saw it as a worker-based nationalist movement that targeted major capitalists as the central enemy. These capitalists were mostly white, although deeply influenced by Jews. White workers were to be rallied into a cohesive force. 'The goal,' he said, 'is a radical change in the system of the United States, a national-socialist system.'" Hitler, Metzger is reported to have said, went after the wrong Jews, the poor ones, not the "big-shots."

But the Nazi element should not be exaggerated. Another important forerunner of current extremist organizations was a man named Gordon Kahl, a folk hero to some farmers in North Dakota, the leader of an anti-tax group called Posse Comitatus. Kahl was convicted of refusing to pay his federal income taxes (which he considered a weapon of Satan and communism), and served eight months in a federal prison. Later, in 1983, he killed three government agents who were attempting to arrest him for probation violation. He was in turn killed after an extensive manhunt. There is considerable information on Kahl and his followers, who were mostly poor farmers in dire financial straits due to the general collapse of small-scale farming in the United States and were threatened with bank foreclosures. The Posse Comitatus (named after the Latin "power of the county") was a transitional group between earlier quasi-Nazi groups and the later militias. Its founder was a retired businessman who had been a member of the Silver Shirts, a Nazi-type organization active in the 1930s. Posse political assumptions were decentralist (no government beyond the county was considered legitimate, a militia theme also), intense racism and anti-Semitism (with some local exceptions), and advocacy of armed resistance to most government authority, hence anti-gun control.

In December 1995 an African-American couple was murdered, apparently by two white soldiers with Nazi sympathies who were stationed at Fort Bragg, North Carolina. This suddenly drew public attention to the existence of numerous white supremacist cliques in the army, even though watchdog organizations had been aware of this for years. There even existed, within the ranks of the Green Beret elite force, a quasi-underground right-wing extremist group that actually published an anti-government newspaper.

Only a few years later, according to a report in the *New York Times* (November 2, 2001), an organization calling itself the "Army of God" sent more than 250 letters to Planned Parenthood offices and abortion providers threatening them with an anthrax attack. It was a hoax. However, a white supremacist convicted of threatening public officials, and vandalizing two synagogues, posted information on the Internet about the use of biological weapons by terrorists, and numerous self-published books and CDs "are virtual cookbooks for anthrax and other biological weapons," the *Times* went on to say. The threat of chemical and biological weapons also should not have come as news. In the mid-1990s there had been a number of incidents involving right-wing extremists accused of plotting to murder federal officials with the toxic compound ricin, or storing ricin or bacteriological materials suitable for causing disease in large numbers of people.

It would be a big mistake to think of right-wing extremists only as swastika-tattooed delinquents, or camouflage-wearing, misguided defenders of small farmers, or as a handful of loose cannon would-be, or even actual, terrorists and assassins. The ultraright is a very broad category. Their particular targets vary; not all are flaming anti-Semites, some overlap with very traditional American anti–big business populist themes going back more than a hundred years. Some are fundamentalist Christian, others are closer to the nihilistic, antireligious attitudes of the Nazi brownshirts of the 1930s.

Indicative of the range of types are two interesting sociological studies. In one, Raphael Ezekiel studied a group of young Detroit Nazis (not, actually, skinheads). Their average age was 19, with the oldest being 30. Most of them were school dropouts, unemployed, unskilled, from "broken" homes characterized by violence, alcoholism, and drug use, often with petty criminal records, and medically unhealthy, living in isolated pockets of whites surrounded by African-American or other racial minorities. In other words, sociologically a marginal group very similar to the German skinheads responsible for the death of the Algerian immigrant.

By contrast, James A. Aho, a sociologist, studied a group of 520 Idaho Christian Patriots, which includes a broad spectrum of theologies, not only the extremist Christian Identity adherents but also other groups for whom Jews are not central to their conspiracy theories. He found this broad population more or less typical of the general population of the area, rather than being the "marginal" types associated with skinheads or the brownshirt wing of the German Nazi Party in Hitler's time. Their average age was 47.6, they had more years of formal education than average Idahoans, most of them were male, they were well-integrated into their communities, their marriages were stable, their occupations did not differ much from most Idahoans except there seemed to be somewhat more independent entrepreneurs and self-employed professionals. There were quite a few "freelance" pastors. Many supported Patrick J. Buchanan's presidential ambitions in 1996 because of Buchanan's focus on corporate greed, his opposition to the North American Free Trade Agreement, and his scapegoating of minorities and immigrants. In short, they are frighteningly normal people in most respects.

There is some disagreement among watchdog groups about whether or not the broad phenomenon of right-wing extremism in organized form is continuing to grow. The number of militia units probably peaked at 858 in 1996, even after the Oklahoma City bombing had scared off many followers, and then declined. Clearly intensified attention by law enforcement agencies played a role. As with other fringe groups of both right and left, there were splits. But perhaps most important, the election of a conservative Republican president in 2000 created a strong impression that a right-wing agenda could successfully be promoted through legitimate political avenues. (Similarly, many German right-wing extremists put their armbands into the closet as it became apparent that they could work successfully inside mainstream conservative parties.) This underlines the fact that there is no clear demarcation between the extremist and mainstream right. Rather, there is a continuum, so that under given circumstances people shift in one direction or the other, and this includes shifting allegiance to particular organizations.

The Internet has seemingly opened up vast opportunities for extremist propaganda because it is so easy to create new groups in cyberspace. There are literally hundreds of right-wing extremist websites (but also dozens of sites for watchdogs). However, this very proliferation makes it harder for single leaders to arise. "The Internet, with its anonymity and lack of physical geography, does not lend itself to bossy leaders or compounds in the woods . . . (it) fuels fragmentation," as Kirk Johnson points out (*New York Times*, April 6, 2005). It is therefore not yet clear whether the Internet will be instrumental in creating a larger right-wing milieu.

There are hundreds of right-wing extremist organizations (many with overlapping memberships). Their most common single denominator (once again, with exceptions) is white supremacism, the notion that the white race is superior, but threatened by various minority "racial" groups, including Jews and many kinds of immigrants. The extreme version of this is the Christian Identity movement. This is a peculiar brand of theology that believes Northern Europeans ("Aryans") are the true Israelites, that Jews are the offspring of Satan, and that people of African descent and others of color are mistakes of creation. Hence Christian Identity is firmly segregationist (and therefore draws Ku Kluxers into its ranks). Politically it advocates a "Christian Republic" based on biblical common law, and denies the legitimacy of most of the U.S. Constitution and law. The Internal Revenue Service, the Federal Reserve Bank, and most other financial organs, public or private (including the World Bank and the International Monetary Fund), it says, are part of a Jewish conspiracy to create a one-world government. Naturally, the *Protocols of the Elders of Zion*, a czarist forgery that is the bedrock document of Jewish conspiracy theories, plays a prominent role.

The more virulent racist and anti-Semitic groups belong to what Chip Berlet of Political Research Associates calls the "extreme right" (*The Public Eye,* Spring 2002). These are "hate groups," defined as those that dehumanize or demonize "members of scapegoated target groups in a systematic way." They foment bigotry as their main or one of their main purposes. Almost all hate groups have more than one target, combining in various degrees hatred of African-Americans, Jews, immigrants of color, and gays. In Europe, in order of importance, it is immigrants, Jews, Gypsies, and gays. The extreme right is also defined by its rejection of democratic institutions, hence these groups are more prepared to use violence against their scapegoat targets and against the legitimate agents of government such as the Internal Revenue Service and even forestry officials. Typical extreme right groups are Christian Identity, the Ku Klux Klan, White Aryan Resistance (WAR), Aryan Nations and its youth auxiliary Youth Action Corps, the National Alliance, and a host of smaller neo-Nazi groups such as Volksfront.

The Jewish conspiracy theme, namely that Jews control international financial institutions, the media, and in the United States, Hollywood (in some versions also using the Freemasons as unwitting stooges) extends far beyond these extreme right circles, even into the literature of some black nationalist organizations. Stephen Eric Bronner, in *A Rumor about the Jews,* tells us that in the 1920s Henry Ford sponsored the publication of *The Protocols of the Elders of Zion* in the United States. James Ridgeway's *Blood in the* Face describes how the Ford-backed newspaper the *Dearborn Independent* promoted the Jewish conspiracy idea in order to discredit everything from the development of commercial practices in the seventeenth century American colonies to the creation of the Federal Reserve Board. There was virtually no institution, or historical development from the French to the Russian revolutions, that was not said to be determined by Jews.

Although there are other conspiracy theories, Jews are almost always implicated. An extreme version is associated with the followers of Lyndon LaRouche, who promote a theory that says the British Crown and the Zionists are responsible for the world drug trade, and that the environmentalist organization Greenpeace was, in Soviet days, controlled by the Soviet secret police, the KGB.

But there are also the more populist conspiracy theories, which involve attacks on the Tri-Lateral Commission, an international policy planning group involving high-level government leaders; the World Bank; and the International Monetary Fund. These are also targets of the Left and of the global justice (or anti-globalization, as it is often wrongly labeled) movement, and unlike extreme right conspiracy theories, they have some basis in empirical reality. There are power structures, they do share memberships, values, and ideas, and they do have considerable control over institutions that can translate values and ideas into policy and practical reality.[1]

In a more polite or code-word form, the Jewish conspiracy idea, rooted in traditional anti-Semitism, is still encountered on a day-to-day basis. In August 2004, Republican House Speaker Dennis Hastert asserted, for example, that financier George Soros, who is of Jewish background and has helped fund democracy-building institutions, especially in the former Soviet bloc countries, got his money from drug cartels. The racism and anti-Semitism of extreme right groups is, in short, only an extreme, overt form of racism and anti-Semitism that exists in much broader segments of the population.

Most of the right, not only the extreme end, also shares with wider parts of the public a moralistic, Manichaean view of the world in black-and-white, good versus evil terms, where good is equated with "traditional values" such as family solidarity, male domination, heterosexuality, hard work, and a fundamentalist and dogmatic Christianity of one kind or another. Often this is connected to what is called "productivism," which is the idea that the population is divided between those who produce (workers, small business people, farmers, and capitalists in the sphere of actual production) and the rest, who are parasites (those on welfare, hippies, students, but also capitalists in the financial sector—especially Jews). This translates into hostility to all those who seem to violate the work ethic, which is part of the constellation of behaviors that make

---

1. But that's the subject for another book. See, for example, G. William Domhoff, *Who Rules America?* (New York: McGraw-Hill, 2002).

up "traditional values." The presumed attack of the nonproductive on those values contributes to xenophobia, fear of the "other" in the interest of protecting or rescuing a white, Christian, hard-working America from immoral forces associated with Jews, dark-skinned foreigners, and African-Americans. Again, code words are employed by the more respectable representatives of conservatism. We are not, they insist, opposed to immigrants, just illegal ones who don't pay taxes (even when they do!). We are not against Jews, we are only against Hollywood's liberal biases (even as the Left attacks Hollywood for its conservative biases!). And we are not racist, we only object to lazy welfare recipients (code word for black).

The logical consequence of this moralistic framework is hostility to the Left and liberalism, which is seen as undermining traditional values by promoting welfare legislation, tolerance, support for the arts, civil rights, women, and gays, not to mention the United Nations and other institutions devoted to negotiation and peaceful resolution of disputes.

Another theme, more common in what Berlet calls the "dissident right" (distinct from "extreme" in that it still places faith in reform of the system) is that of opposition to a strong central state, not just the current "corrupt" or "treasonous" or "Jewish-Communist dominated" one. Hence opposition to gun control, taxes, public schools (engendering support for the home schooling movement), environmental legislation, regulation of business, and even military conscription (only citizen militias or sheriffs' posses at the local level are seen as legitimate). Much of this is based on "constitutionalism," the theory that only the original U.S. Constitution is valid, and that most other legislation is un-Christian and should be resisted. The extreme is "survivalism," which advocates total withdrawal from U.S. society to either one Christian state (Idaho? Oregon?) or even beyond that to armed Christian, racially "pure" communes.

The dissident right, in Berlet's typology, came out of the economic plight of rural areas in the early 1990s, and includes the broadly defined "Christian Right" (including Reverend Pat Robertson's Christian Coalition and many other dogmatic evangelical groups), and the broad "Patriot movements," which spun off the militias. The Christian Right framework combines a set of reactionary social policies, most of them negative: anti–gay rights, anti-feminism, anti-abortion, anti–gun control, anti-evolution and above all against the separation of church and state. The Christian Right is in favor of putting religion back into the public schools, returning autonomy to families (permitting corporal punishment and especially returning authority to men, as with the overwhelmingly white male movement called "Promise Keepers"). The Patriot, sometimes called Christian Patriot, segments overlap with the Christian Right, but place more emphasis on individual liberties and the belief that secret elites are manipulating the government. Their core is in Idaho and eastern Washington.

These are the small-scale property owners and independent professionals studied by James Aho. According to the watchdog group Political Research Associates, some five million Americans were involved with Patriot social movements in 2002.

Representatives of the Christian Right today have considerable political power, as anyone observing the rhetoric, and the policy advocacies, of the Bush administration must realize. President Bush's first attorney general, John Ashcroft, is generally identified with this movement. Obviously there is a fundamental contradiction here: the attempted centralization of police powers under Ashcroft, accompanied by increasing restrictions on civil liberties, flies in the face of the libertarianism advocated by the Patriot movement, and has in fact made for some unlikely allies as conservative libertarians join with the very symbol of liberalism, the American Civil Liberties Union, to protest infringements on the Bill of Rights.

The broad "hard right" (Berlet's term) movement including both extreme and dissident wings can be differentiated in terms of four issues, as we have seen: 1) the degree of racism/anti-Semitism; 2) the degree of rigid adherence to traditional morality; 3) the degree of hostility toward a strong central state; 4) the degree of hostility towards corporate capitalism (the populism dimension); and 5) the degree to which people are prepared to use violence in pursuit of their aims. In the United States, which is, it must be remembered, the most moralistic (not the same as moral) nation in the world, the majority of what is called the political Right is moralistic, Manichaean (sees the world in black-white, good-evil terms) libertarian (anti-state), racist and anti-Semitic, and, if anti-corporate, not anti-capitalist as such. Anti-corporatism is anti-finance capital, specifically anti-Jewish finance capital, just as the Nazis emphasized.

Manichaeanism (named after a third-century Persian who combined several religious, including Christian, elements to teach a doctrine based on the two contending principles of good and evil, God versus Satan) seems to be a common denominator of the supremacist, moralistic, simplistically populist, and potentially violent adherents of the ultra or hard right. There is a generalized hostility toward those who are perceived to be outsiders (non-white, Jews), immoral slackers, nonproductive elite conspirators, and those who politically support these elements (liberals and the Left, in theory in control of the government). This attitude, a number of social scientists have argued, is correlated to a type of personality that has been labeled "authoritarian." Seymour Martin Lipset, in his well-known book *Political Man,* tells us that lower income, working-class individuals are more authoritarian than middle class and better educated people. This has been vigorously debated over the years, especially given the fact that wealthy people vote disproportionally for right-wing candidates for office—and in Germany that included Hitler. Nevertheless, there is something to the idea that such a personality type does exist in all classes. Lipset and many others attribute the development of this personality to childhood experience, or socialization, in which a punitive family environment involving lack of love and considerable aggression and conflict plays an important part. This leads, in Lipset's words, to "a tendency to view politics and personal relationships in black-and-white terms, a desire for immediate action, an impatience with talk and discussion, a lack of interest in organizations which have a long-range perspective, and a readiness to follow leaders who offer a demonological interpretation of the evil forces (either religious or political) which are conspiring against him."

What are some of the other characteristics of "the authoritarian personality," or the Manichaean worldview? Dogmatism and a low level of tolerance for ambiguity would naturally be part of this view. The individual needs the security of believing in a set of ideas that are unchallengeable in this rapidly changing, insecure world. He or she needs the "island of safety" that is represented by a firm framework that is questioned only by the "others," those against whom one's identity is established. The very fact that the "others" challenge this framework confirms that it is true. It follows that this personality type is less open to complex thinking, more ready to accept simple slogans. There are many "content analyses" of speeches and writings of right wing versus liberal and left-wing sources that confirm this empirically. The "sound bite" approach to political commentary on television, the short snappy political speech rather than the contemplative, reflective one with nuances suit the right-wing personality better than the left.

Another characteristic of this personality is the need for order and structure, a logical component of the need for security. In surveys that test for prejudice and the authoritarianism that is often at its root, the agree-disagree question is: "It would be better if teachers were more strict"; or, "We do not have enough discipline in our American way of life" (from Allport), or the classical one, "What this country needs is a few strong, courageous, hard-working leaders in whom the people can put their faith" (from *The Authoritarian Personality,* the pioneering study by Theodor W. Adorno and his colleagues, published in 1950).

The authoritarian personality sees the world as a dangerous place full of conspiracies. Generally social change of whatever kind is seen as a threat to traditional values, from scientific theories such as evolution to social policies such as the integration of gays and lesbians into the armed forces. The demagogue or the right-wing organization promises to combat that threat and restore what is believed to have been a stable, secure society.

Another personality dimension that coincides with the authoritarian mentality, although it is also present in a much wider sector of the population, is an intense "machismo," or extreme parading of masculinity to the point of male supremacy. This machismo is ingrained quite early in life as part of male role socialization for many men, but it may also become intensified as men find their roles relatively diminished with the increased economic and political power of women, and as gays become more publicly accepted. Machismo can be traced to the family structure of patriarchy, a form that is historically rooted in agrarian life going back to the Old Testament. The agrarian American frontier family was generally patriarchal in form (unless the male head of the household had died, perhaps killed). Beginning just before the Civil War, if not earlier, the frontier farmer was very often armed. Conservatives tend to romanticize traditional small-town, rural America, where men were men, had guns, and women knew their place. Hence their antipathy to gun control and their near obsession with images of good gunfighters righting wrongs, Clint Eastwood-style, with or without the blessing of the law. The strong, virile rural American male is an image that many politicians attempt to copy as they seek the support of conservative voters who, by definition, look back to the "good old days" for inspiration and comfort. Note the body image of President George Bush, who, perhaps quite unconsciously, walks with his arms slightly away from his body, just like the proverbial gunfighter.

It needs to be pointed out that many children suffer from lack of love and are victims of punitive parents, yet they do not develop into right-wing fanatics. Many men grow up in small towns and on farms and do not walk around with gun in hand, nor do they aspire to do so. Many conservatives do not hanker to have a strong leader take charge of their lives, quite the contrary. Cooperativism rather than macho individualism remains an alternative framework for many people who live in the states normally thought of as bastions of right-wing politics. Socialization is never uniform in any sector of the population.

Even for those predisposed to authoritarian thinking, that alone is an insufficient explanation for hard right political allegiances. Real life experiences including downward economic mobility (the loss of jobs, farms) and social status (the perceived loss of white privilege, white neighborhoods, male domination, the threat to "American values" from immigrants, and so on) interact with a person's socialization to produce what is no more than a *tendency* to think in Manichaean terms, a vulnerability to ultraright-wing thinking. A set of simple messages from right-wing organizations plays to the predisposition. But a third factor also needs to enter the picture: a political vacuum in which an ultraright organization can become a major factor.

So this is the formula: 1) Predisposition rooted in socialization; 2) social conditions (insecurities, rapid social change, downward mobility); 3) a simple message (the displacement of blame onto a scapegoat group, conspiracy theories); 4) a failure of alternative messages (normally more complex, involving long-term policies); 5) resources devoted to right-wing organizations; all these leading to 6) a viable movement.

Large-scale funding from conservative foundations does not normally go directly into the coffers of ultraright-wing organizations. It goes mainly to conservative think tanks and policy planning organizations such as the Heritage Foundation, the American Enterprise Institute, the Cato Institute, or the Pioneer Fund. There are a dozen or more foundations that fund a broad array of conservative educational and "research" efforts, including the publication of books by conservative authors, as in the *Bell Curve* instance.

Heritage, which is primarily devoted to policy formation and dissemination, was founded in 1973 by the notoriously anti-labor and anti-civil rights beer baron Joseph Coors. By 1995 Heritage had an annual budget of $25 million. It is supported directly or indirectly via charitable foundations by dozens of corporations. In 2002 it received more than $10 million from the Bradley, Scaife, Carthage, Castle Rock, Olin, Lambe, Hume, DeVos, Roe, Donner, Grewcock, and McKenna foundations, most of which was not earmarked for specific programs. Some of the personnel from such institutions and foundations have attained important government positions, especially in Republican administrations, and in turn government officials sit on the boards of such organizations. Institutions such as Heritage have, over the past several decades, succeeded in moving the general ideology of the country to the right, and that in turn has made many ultraright causes more respectable. They support an ideological framework that provides the talking points used by the hard right.

How do those opposed to the general perspective of the very broad conservative movement propose to answer the real threat if not the actuality of a conservative takeover of our institutions and culture? More specifically, how do they propose to deal with the more dangerous ultra or hard right, especially the extreme right? The answer to the first is beyond the scope of this book, although it is implied when we talk about the fears, real and imagined, of those who are in economic trouble and whose status is challenged by the rapid social changes all about them. More about this in the final chapter of this book. It is the hard right that concerns us in this chapter.

The best-known and most public line of defense against the ultraright consists of a set of watchdog groups that has been observing and publicizing the activities of the extreme right for many years. The dominant strategy of mainstream liberal watchdog groups is to publicize, and perhaps scare. This is intended to put pressure on politicians and on police agencies to enforce laws, and some would extend this to passing new restrictive measures such as hate-crime laws (which would put U.S. legislation more in line with European and Canadian legislation, but run counter to "free speech and association" provisions of the U.S. Constitution). Scare stories also serve the purpose of fund-raising.

The problem here is twofold: first, as we well know, justice is blind in its right eye. Historically there has been much police collusion with the right, especially in the South with the KKK. Indeed, there have been numerous instances where local police were actually KKK members. A number of extremist leaders today are former police officers or armed forces veterans, including former officers. Second, when the state does finally intervene (in the interest of its own security), it overreacts and creates martyrs, as in the Waco, Texas shootout involving the Branch Davidians, a survivalist sect, and other cases in the recent past.

Another shortcoming of the "publicize and educate" approach is that it is difficult, to put it mildly, to gain serious access to the media in the face of an overwhelming deluge of hate spewing forth from radio talk shows hosted by racist, sexist, anti-Semitic, and homophobic hosts. Moreover, corporate control of the media has shrunk and redefined the terms of the debate between Left and Right in such a way as to exclude serious progressive voices. The cancellation of left-populist Jim Hightower's talk show is an example. The effort to create alternative media is laudable but runs into financial problems. There are a few successful cable TV shows (*The Daily Show* with Jon Stewart is a good example), and a radio network, Air America, that present alternative progressive political messages, but in the large scheme of things they are a distinct minority.

A different strategy is to try to bankrupt extremist organizations by bringing civil lawsuits. The Southern Poverty Law Center has taken this approach quite successfully probably as far as it can go. In 1979 the Center sued the Klan in civil court when the FBI failed to find sufficient evidence for a criminal case after the disruption of a civil rights march in Decatur, Alabama. The case was settled in 1990 with the Klan paying some damages. The Klansmen involved were also required to attend a course on race relations and prejudice. In 1981 the Center sued a different unit of the Klan on behalf of Vietnamese-American fishermen after armed Klan members burned their boats. The Center claims that the suit shut down the Klan's paramilitary training bases. Better known was the 1988 case of the White Aryan Resistance. Portland, Oregon skinheads recruited and trained by WAR attacked and killed an Ethiopian student. The Center sued, and in 1990 a jury awarded $12.5 million to the family of the victim. An appeal to the U.S. Supreme Court failed, and in 1994 WAR's assets were sold off and the proceeds began to be paid. In 1991 the Center won a judgment against a white supremacist group called the Church of the Creator, a member of which had murdered a black sailor. The Church transferred ownership of its headquarters to a neo-Nazi named William Pierce, who headed a group called the National Alliance. The Center sued Pierce and eventually won $85,000. In 1998 the Center brought a suit against the Christian

Knights of the KKK on behalf of the Macedonia (South Carolina) Baptist Church, one of several black churches burned by arsonists in the mid-1990s. The Klan unit was ordered to pay $21.5 million, the largest judgment to date, which forced it to sell its headquarters and go out of business.

A more interesting case was one involving the Aryan Nations. In 1998 a guard at their complex in Idaho shot at two people after their car backfired outside. The Center sued on their behalf and ultimately won a $6.3 judgment against Aryan Nations and its leader, Richard Butler. The organization was forced to give up its twenty-acre property, which was turned into a community peace park.

Apart from the problem that such suits take time, these legalistic strategies, since they deal with symptoms only, can be successful only in the short run. Organizations come and go in the extreme right milieu anyway, so when one or two are bankrupted, they can if they desire go underground, change names, and reappear. This strategy is incapable of destroying extremism, nor does it claim to do more than make it more difficult for extremist organizations to function. It does put some pressure on law enforcement agencies, however, since it is somewhat embarrassing when the police or FBI fail to bring a criminal case, and a civilian agency manages to win judgments.

The scare tactics used by the Center via its magazine, *Intelligence Report,* involve a problematic methodological approach common to most watchdog groups: the long listings, and counts, of apparent hate crimes without differentiating among them. A National Alliance flyer distributed in some town, a harassing phone call, a racial slur painted on a building, four teenagers vandalizing a church—each one an incident to be counted alongside much more serious incidents involving, for example, aggravated assault and battery against several gay men, or members of an actual extremist group called Skinhead East Coast Hate Crew beating a Latino with a bat. If the purpose is to scare us (and who would not be scared by photograph after photograph of youths parading in black shirts with swastikas, no matter how tiny the organization?) these enumerations also divert us from a serious analysis of the reasons for such behavior. What kind of people are involved? What are their backgrounds? What are their motivations? Serious research on these questions is still scarce, and watchdog organizations commit few resources to this end.

Another strategy is conversion (or, social work in the case of Nazi skinhead gangs). This approach is more common in European countries, especially in Germany. Individual conversion, although it has been known to work in a few cases, takes too long. Social work or gang work requires financial resources at the very time such resources are being cut. Moreover, very few street workers are effective at this, the exception being the totalitarian Nation of Islam, which has had some success with black "underclass" and prison populations.

There are some success stories from other countries, but this approach is not used in the United States to any significant extent.

The limited success of the Nation of Islam suggests still another strategy: that of creating militant action groups that would be, in effect, militaristic alternatives to right-wing formations. Such groups might also engage in street battles and attacks on right extremist meetings and marches. In the 1920s and early 1930s the German Communist and Socialist Parties organized such paramilitary auxiliaries to fight the Nazis. There are no such groups on the horizon, one reason being that the very thought of a necessarily undemocratic militaristic formation that would engage in street battles is completely foreign to current U.S. progressive forces, with the exception of one or two tiny left wing sects. Moreover, physical attacks on extremist marches play directly into the hands of the extremists in that they enable them to play the martyr role and provide terrific publicity. In any case, the right is far better at fighting, and much better trained.

A more promising strategy is that of community resistance. This requires the collaboration of "mainstream" ministers and a range of other community activists in a movement intended to demonstrate widespread support for a different and more tolerant version of "the American way of life" than that promoted by the ultraright. In effect, this strategy, which includes educational programs as well as large meetings and public rallies, makes extremism politically unwelcome in a community.

"Not in Our Town" is a national organization that has pioneered this strategy. It began in Billings, Montana in 1993, when residents who had attended a Martin Luther King Jr. birthday celebration found racist literature on their cars. Then the Jewish cemetery was vandalized, the home of a Native-American named Dawn Fast Horse was painted with swastikas, and several Jews had bricks or bottles thrown into their homes. Community members got into action. First, the local Painters Union repainted Dawn Fast Horse's home. Candlelight vigils and a "Stand Together Billings" rally took place. The local newspaper printed a full-page replica of a Menorah, the Jewish candlestick used during the Hanukkah celebration each year, and this was displayed in nearly 10,000 homes and businesses.

The attacks continued, however. Bricks were thrown through the windows of a school and into two churches that had put up the Menorah, and others displaying it got anti-Semitic phone calls. Several cars were vandalized. The police chief, Wayne Inman, took a strong and visible position against these acts. He had, in fact, been on the police force in Portland, Oregon at the time of the Aryan Nations murder, and had become convinced that a community response could succeed in thwarting further attacks. Apparently he was right because the attacks soon stopped and have not resumed. The "Not in Our Town" idea subsequently spread to a number of other communities that had suffered racist attacks at the hands of right-extremist groups.

Since September 11, 2001, anti-immigrant sentiment, initially fueled by hostility to people of Middle Eastern and Asian backgrounds stereotyped as Islamic terrorists, has been on the rise. But this was soon extended to all immigrants of color, especially the undocumented, or illegals, most of whom are from Mexico. Under the rationale of preventing terrorists from crossing our borders, and the cover of the Patriot Act, the government has taken a much harsher stand on immigration law enforcement. Right-wing extremist groups have jumped into the fray: immigrants in general, and the illegals in particular, have become a major scapegoat target. Conveniently, immigrants fit several stereotypes that have been a historical constant in anti-immigrant hysteria: they are undermining the sanctity of the white race, they commit crimes, they threaten "our" jobs, they use up "our" scarce resources, they give birth to too many illegitimate children, they foster drug-peddling gangs (in the mid-1800s alcohol was the issue), and best (or worst) of all, some of them are potential terrorists. For a number of right-wing extremist groups whose websites can be viewed on the Internet, immigrants have virtually displaced African-Americans and Jews as the major targets nowadays. One such group, United Patriots of America, promotes a program called "Let's Take Back America," which identifies "illegal alien trespassers" as one of America's major problems. They link to the Federation for American Immigrant Reform, which holds that "the threads that hold this large and diverse country are being threatened" by immigrants. They also link to the "English Only" movement and to the Minuteman Project, a vigilante group "patrolling" the Arizona-Mexico border in order to catch illegals crossing into the United States, a campaign that has been condemned by most law enforcement agencies. There is no mention of white supremacy, indeed of any of the usual right-wing extremist themes. Nevertheless, much current anti-immigrant propaganda is a continuation of a historic xenophobic message that fits all too well into the broad spectrum of right-wing politics. It provides encouragement to less extreme conservative forces intent on preventing more liberal immigration policies.

Immigrant rights groups have emerged to counter this political attack, as mentioned in the previous chapter. The focus of defense groups has been to emphasize the humanitarian and civil libertarian side of the issue, and to try to counter some of the lies spread about undocumented immigrants. Yet this as well as other strategies mentioned in this chapter are defensive, that is, they deal with actions that have taken place, or they try to deter or prevent actions that are believed imminent. They publicize past events in order to alert that part of the public that supports civil rights and liberties and fears extremism. But in the long run a strategy must be developed that will create a progressive populist alternative to the right-wing agenda. Attention must be shifted from con-spiracies focusing on minorities, to those social and economic forces that are really responsible for the malaise of so many individuals. The militant traditions of American progressive populism a century ago, and the socialist movement as it existed in the lifetime of Eugene Victor Debs, suggest that militant dem-ocratic alternative messages have the potential of resonating even with sectors of the hard right.

· 6 ·

Terror(ism) and Hatred:
"Why Do They Hate Us?"

$\mathcal{W}$hat is terrorism? Who is a terrorist? Do terrorists hate? These are complex questions that have been debated since the French Revolution, when the term *terror* in the modern sense was probably first used. The "Reign of Terror" refers to the 1793–1794 period when the revolutionary government under Robespierre guillotined some 2,500 Royalists, others suspected of subversion, and some economic criminals such as food speculators. Initially, then, it was a government rather than what we term "nonstate actors" that attempted (successfully in this case) to terrorize a sufficient number of its domestic enemies so as to crush counterrevolutionary or criminal elements. The key to this success was its randomness: one never knew who would be next, or exactly why one was being picked out, a lesson Stalin learned all too well.

Most people, however, associate terrorism with nonstate actors, individuals or groups using violence to assassinate public figures, or to kill larger numbers of people out of some political or religious motive, sometimes as part of a larger campaign to overthrow a government. Until probably around the 1930s terrorism was, in the public mind, virtually synonymous with anarchism, since anarchists or groups that could somehow be connected to anarchism, even if incorrectly, were responsible for attacks, including suicidal ones, against a number of crowned and uncrowned heads of state or other individuals implicated in some presumed oppressive role in the society. Warren Billings and Tom Mooney, two labor organizers convicted of planting a bomb at a Preparedness Day parade in San Francisco in 1916 that killed ten people, were not accused of being terrorists. Rather, the assistant district attorney prosecuting the case called them "dirty anarchists" and advocated they be taken out and lynched. They were ultimately pardoned after many years in prison, mainly because more and more evidence turned up showing they were framed.

71

The behaviors that have been labeled terrorism are almost as numerous as the definitions. For example, on September 5, 1972, eight Palestinians infiltrated the Olympic Village in Munich, Germany, seized eleven Israeli athletes and coaches, and after German police bungled an effort to free the hostages, killed all the Israelis. Five Palestinian terrorists also died. Many years later, in June, 2004, twenty-five families of the deceased divided $3.6 million in compensation from the German government. For the Palestine Liberation Organization, which appeared to be responsible for the attack, the perpetrators were freedom fighters, part of a war against Israel, and not terrorists.

On July 22, 1946, during the British Mandate in Palestine, the Jewish underground organization Irgun, headed by Menachem Begin, who would later become Prime Minister of Israel, blew up a wing of the King David Hotel in Jerusalem. It housed the British military command and its intelligence files. The Irgun had telephoned warnings that were ignored. Ninety-one people died. The British called it terrorism. The Irgun called it part of a war for independence.

During the night of May 16–17, 1943, 17 Lancaster bombers of the Royal Air Force attacked and destroyed the Möhne Dam, a few kilometers from the Westfalian town of Soest in Germany (where the author happens to have been born). The dam was a source of electric energy that helped power Ruhr industrial production. A huge flood hit several villages below the dam, drowning some 1,300 people, many of them Ukrainian women and children trapped in a German prisoner of war camp. Of the 17 bombers, only eight survived. The squadron leader was awarded the Victoria Cross. Within a month the dam had been repaired, and within the year steel production in the Ruhr valley had doubled. The dam bombing took place during a period of "terror bombing," to use Winston Churchill's expression, of German cities intended to undermine morale and turn the population against Hitler.

The strategy of terror bombing began with the bombing of Guernica in northern Spain by German aircraft on April 27, 1937, killing some 1,600 civilians. This was followed by the bombing of Rotterdam on May 14, 1940, killing about 900. In the latter case the bombing was explicitly designed to force the Dutch to surrender, which they were in the process of doing even as the bombing commenced. Terror bombing got worse after that. The Allied bombing of Dresden on February 13, 1945, killed about 35,000 people. On March 9 of that same year, as the end of the war was approaching, some 300 B-29 bombers attacked Tokyo, killing around 84,000 people. In the atom bombings of Hiroshima and Nagasaki on August 6 and 9, about 66,000 people, one-fourth of the population of Hiroshima, died almost instantly and a similar number were injured. In Nagasaki, about 39,000 people died. In all these cases the vast majority of the victims were civilians. Since that time, as C. Douglas Lummis points out in a recent essay, new terror weapons have been devised and used. Richard Gatling, were he alive, would be astonished at the latest version of his machine gun. It can fire up to 6,000 rounds a minute and can "fill an area the size of a football field with one round per square foot." It is fired from an AC-130 cargo plane, which also fires cannon. "We hear that part of its utility is the terrifying effect of the deafening sound of its huge propeller engines combined with the boom of the howitzer coming from high in the sky." The notion that such weapons are used only against legitimate military targets "is belied by the very nature of the weapons: the intention to 'kill all' is designed into them. . . . The people who drop these bombs [a variety of cluster bombs that scatter munitions over very wide areas] drop them with the intention of killing everybody who's down there."

The above examples, all of which explicitly or implicitly involve the term terrorism, represent quite a range of violent behavior, some carried out by individual actors, others by "state actors," that is, governments via their military. In every one of these examples the argument has been made that these were acts carried out in the course of a justifiable war. Underground fighters using tactics such as bombings with or without casualties, or even carefully targeted assassination, have uniformly been accused of terrorism (or, in an earlier period, anarchism), and have uniformly justified their actions, no matter how heinous they seem to us, as legitimate acts of war intended as part of a war to overcome an evil enemy. The same justification is uniformly used for the bombing of cities even though most of the casualties are civilians and even when the military value of the city is close to nil (that is, when there are few or no industrial facilities, railroad intersections, military barracks, or other installations).

The attacks on the World Trade Center and the Pentagon on September 11, 2001, made the term terrorism a household word. Yet even here the label is debatable. The Twin Towers were virtually *the* symbol of the U.S. role as the administrative center of world capitalism and imperialism. As such some people undoubtedly saw them as legitimate targets of the war against empire and the Western culture of Enlightenment that had led to the colonization and impoverishment of much of the world. However, even if some of those working in the WTC were complicit, thousands of others had nothing to do with that. The random deaths of innocent civilians defined that as terrorism. On the other hand, irregular nonstate forces seeing themselves at war with the United States could logically view the Pentagon as a legitimate military target. Civilian employees of the Pentagon knowingly work for the military; employees of financial services companies, or of the Windows on the World restaurant in the World Trade Center were no more guilty of complicity with evil than any employee of any institution in the United States.

Given this range of "terrorist" actions, can we at least come close to a common denominator definition? There seems to be a broad consensus that the key to a definition of terrorism is the randomness of its victims, and that its objective is to terrorize rather than specifically to select targets such as individuals to kill or buildings or bridges to destroy. By this definition an assassin is not a terrorist; the label is applied to discredit the perpetrator. On August 24, 1970, in the midst of the Vietnam War, an explosion destroyed the Army Mathematics Research Center at the University of Wisconsin in Madison. There had been a telephone warning to vacate the building, but one man was killed in the blast. This was an act of sabotage intended to interfere with the American war effort, in the same way that the King David Hotel bombing was specifically aimed at the war making capability of the British army. By contrast, the Oklahoma City bombing, although symbolically targeting a federal government building, killed 167 people, including 19 children in a day care center. It can justifiably be called terrorism.

But what is the purpose of such random terror? It is to coerce people (including governments) to change their policies. That is, it has as its objective the preventing or halting of some action, or somehow changing the direction of events (perhaps by coercing a government to change its policies). Of course this can be done by means short of random terror. It could involve the physical elimination of one or more persons (by assassination), or by sabotage, kidnappings, beatings, mutilations, cross-burnings, and other forms of harassment (the objective being the social control or even the elimination of a minority, perhaps). It could involve vigilantism (when communities "take the law into their own hands"). Vigilante actions include night riders (the Ku Klux Klan), mob lynchings, death squads (paramilitaries torturing and executing targeted victims), and pogroms (mob, military, or paramilitary invasions of ethnic neighborhoods with attendant beatings, murder, rape, and destruction of property). All of these and more have been labeled terrorism at one time or another.

If we include all of these tactics in the definition, terrorism can be one of a panoply of tactics in a wider underground resistance movement or a guerrilla movement. In these tactical forms it is sometimes the first stage of the development of broader revolutionary movements. The terrorist's objective may be more to raise political awareness than to inflict injury or destruction.

The common denominator of all of these behaviors is violence with the intention of coercing a change in policy (either by preventing or stopping an action, or forcing a different and new action). Yet as we tack more kinds of violent behavior (sabotage, assassination, guerrilla warfare) onto the definition, it loses precision and becomes vulnerable to political manipulation. A stingy definition is safer: terrorism is violence carried out by individuals, groups, or nations via its military forces directed indiscriminately against a population in order to obtain a change in policy. Bombing, starvation of vulnerable populations, the deliberate spread of disease, large-scale random "disappearances," systematic large-scale rape, and mass executions are the weapons of choice.

Terrorism is often used as a label applied to certain criminal acts when states, or the media or other institutions, don't like the actor's politics or religion. In today's world insurgents, rebels, revolutionaries, guerrillas, para-militaries, and others have been relabeled terrorists when it became politically convenient. Terrorism carries with it a heavily negative connotation. This point was made clear in September 2004, when a Canadian newspaper chain ordered the substitution of the word "terrorist" for "insurgent" and "rebel." The Reuters news agency, which supplies some of the news to this chain, objected, saying it does not use "emotive" words like terrorist when describing someone. It asked that if the newspaper chain insisted, Reuters' reporters' bylines be omitted, partly for their own safety when covering news in war-torn areas.

The labeling of groups, including those engaged in peaceful protests, sit-ins, throwing eggs at buildings, or using stink bombs, as terrorists by the state and the media magnifies their importance and generates public hysteria, which in turn is manipulated in order to enact emergency laws, invasive surveillance, and increased police powers in general. When even minor symbolic acts of violence against property are criminalized and dealt with by the police in the harshest manner, some activists move to real violence on the principle that if one is going to prison anyway, it might as well be for something serious. This was in part what happened in Germany in the 1970s, when some elements of the student movement went underground and resorted to kidnapping and killing. The state had created a self-fulfilling prophecy by throwing the net of the terrorist label over so many different levels of behavior, and using the police indiscriminately against them.

At the international level, the terrorist label is applied to just about any form of armed uprising considered dangerous to the status quo, or to U.S. interests (often the same thing) even when they differ in fundamental ways and are indeed hostile to one another. When such diverse groups as the Sandinistas of Nicaragua, the Colombian FARC, the Maoists of Nepal and India, the Peruvian Shining Path and that country's Tupac Amaru guerrilla movements, as well as Mexico's insurgent peasant Zapatista movement in Chiapas are all labeled terrorist, this is a useful way for a government to dismiss and discredit any movement opposing oppression, including those that condemn violence.

It is useful for the state to promote the terrorism label when it wishes to develop a strategy of strengthening social control mechanisms. Civil liberties are undermined by shortcutting judicial proceedings, moving them from civilian to military courts, imprisoning suspects without judicial proceedings for long periods, preventing suspects from having access to attorneys, and sentencing them, with or without judicial proceedings, to unusually long periods of imprisonment in unusually harsh conditions. The general population, frightened by the specter of terrorism, tends to acquiesce.

But there is a second function for this process. Labeling acts as terrorist switches attention from causes to acts. That is, the terrorist act becomes the focus of public attention, and attention to its underlying causes is deflected. For example, a movement for national independence that takes a violent form (armed insurrection, guerrilla warfare) is labeled terrorism. This refocuses our attention from the problem of ethnic or national subordination that has resulted in an armed insurgency (say, in Chechnya or Palestine) to the terrifying label of terrorist activity. Revolutionary activity, or perhaps a movement for national independence, becomes redefined as a heinous crime. This is important for those in power because attention to underlying causes would inevitably end with an indictment, at least in part, of the institutions that have created the fertile soil for the rise of extremist movements of whatever flavor or color.

Even when an act is terrorism in the narrower definition of the term, emphasis on that designation makes it harder to look rationally at causes. The atmosphere after September 11, 2001, made it virtually impossible to publicly discuss the historical background that might have contributed to the formation of these terrorist cells. To do so sounded too much like making excuses for the terrorists. Instead, the terrorists were loosely linked to an undifferentiated Islam. It was widely assumed, and even argued in some academic circles, that there was a clash of civilizations, and that the "other" civilization (that is, Islam) was indirectly if not directly responsible for this terrorism, which was allegedly targeting "our" Judeo-Christian civilization.

The casualties caused by terrorists, no matter how many and how painful, are comparatively very few compared to official, legally sanctioned terror. An example of state terror is the deliberate starvation of a population, as in Ireland during the potato famine. Other examples come all too readily to mind in this century: the brutalization of a population through poverty; child labor; slavery; the expulsion of a people from their lands; genocide based on religious, political, ethnic, and sexual identities; aerial bombardment; police brutality; official torture; the prison system in general and capital punishment in particular, and the systematic violence done by industry by way of pollution and the manufacture of dangerous products, quite apart from its superexploitation of workers by paying so many of them, worldwide, below-subsistence-level wages. To paraphrase the late sociologist Alfred McClung Lee from his last book, *Terrorism in Northern Ireland*, more terrorists wear three-piece suits, ride in Rolls-Royces, and sit in the seats of corporate power and government than lurk in dark alleys.

At one level, as some pacifists argue, all terrorism is violent (and perhaps all violence is terrorism) and therefore equally reprehensible. However, distinctions can and should be drawn. Sabotage (from the French word for a wooden shoe, *sabot,* that workers were said to have thrown into the new weaving machines that were creating widespread unemployment) should be excluded if it is carefully directed and solely aimed at property. The damaging of draft board files or missile components as part of an antiwar campaign, while illegal, is nonviolent in that the consequent suffering, if any, is undertaken solely by the perpetrator when that person is caught and imprisoned. This is clearly not the case for those who bomb abortion clinics because they disregard the danger of death or injury to persons, including uninvolved bystanders. The same is true for suicide bombers in Israel or Russia who use themselves to blow up random buses, trains, or airplanes, killing civilians not directly implicated in any of the activities the bombers are protesting. It is important, however, to remember that in all of these cases the criminals believe that their cause is just, and labeling them as terrorists does not help us to understand that cause. Of course understanding a cause does not mean we have to agree with it. Such an understanding can, however, help us to evaluate the possibilities of resolving an issue or a conflict. This is less likely when we use the terrorism label as an emotionally-laden shortcut description of an event.

What is the connection between terrorism and hate? It is often assumed that terrorists must hate their victims, for otherwise how would they be able to undertake the kind of widespread and random killing for which they are known, or, even worse, for which they are willing to commit suicide? In the op-ed columns we are told that the massacre of innocents, as in the case of the schoolchildren in Beslan, Russia, in 2004, is attributable to a "death cult that is thriving at the fringes of the Muslim world," that the terrorists kill "for the sheer pleasure of killing and dying . . . the joy of sadism and suicide," that such terrorist groups constitute a "pathological mass movement" (David Brooks in the *New York Times*, September 7, 2004).

There is no evidence for such extreme statements. They only serve to obscure any underlying causes for these horrifying attacks. The term *pathology* is used to "medicalize" or "psychiatrize" behavior so that we can dismiss it as insane. This absolves all other parties from any culpability. It is not at all clear that even those terrorists who engage in random, large-scale murder by means of suicide bombing "hate" their anonymous victims, much less that they constitute a death cult or that they are mental cases. It is not clear that assassins necessarily hate their victims. Even the perpetrators of war crimes against innocent civilians do not necessarily hate their victims on a personal level. There is no evidence that terrorists are in any way abnormal, psychopathic, or indeed psychologically or emotionally different from whatever the standard of normality is in a given society. The man who assassinated President James McKinley in 1901, Leon Czolgosz, is said to have been a modest man whose act was one of vengeance for the massacre of some miners in Pennsylvania. On close examination it turns out that most assassinations have been acts of revenge for prior acts of terror against some oppressed population. It seems to be the case that Chechnya women suicide bombers termed "black widows" act to take vengeance for the deaths of relatives at the hands of Russian security forces. This is tragic, but it is not insane.

In chapter 2, one of the examples of "hate" was that of the German police unit that executed some 1,800 Jewish civilians in Poland. We assume that these Germans hated the Jews. Yet when we look more closely, as Christopher R. Browning did in his book *Ordinary Men*, we find the situation more complicated. After the war there were extensive hearings about this atrocity. The commanding officer, a major, offered his men the chance not to participate in this murderous assignment, and some dozen, including an officer who was a member of the Nazi Party, refused the assignment. The major himself was apparently psychologically incapable of witnessing the executions, and witnesses testified that he wept openly. But orders were orders, and they were carried out, however reluctantly. However horrendous and inexcusable the event, it is hard to make the case that hate was involved except on the part of one or two of the soldiers.

The assumption that states terrorize for rational motives and individuals act on the basis of emotion is wrong both ways. States terrorize on the basis of motives that may not, in fact, be rational: the outcomes of state terrorism have unanticipated "blow-back" effects that increase hostility to the perpetrator, and unify the population rather than demoralize it, as in many instances of aerial bombardment (short of nuclear weapons). Individuals terrorize on the basis of motives that are quite rational even though they too have blow-back effects that call that rationality into question. But hatred, except on the very general level of hatred for a system, or hatred of oppression, or of imperialism, or of poverty, is not the trigger. Revenge for the death of family members, or co-religionists, or worker comrades, is often a factor in the recruitment of potential terrorists. In earlier times, and even today, insults or the demeaning of a man's female family member or a group's women have resulted in acts of revenge, but these acts were not so much based on hatred as on a calculated attempt to maintain a certain kind of social order. They were rarely if ever called terrorism.

We should assume that in general terrorists act for rational reasons as they see them, and not on the basis of emotion, much less mental instability. We often think, after a terrorist attack, that they must have been quite mad to believe the act would alter events in any way beneficial to them. Yet as a society or a government reacts to terrorism by intense repression of the population from which the terrorists have sprung, more terrorists (or revolutionaries) are often born. The rule seems to be: in a population that generally believes its government to be legitimate and responsive, terrorists seeing themselves as precursors of revolution are ultimately doomed providing that police action does not unduly oppress the innocent. But terrorists (or bandits, or guerrillas) find shelter and opportunity in a population that believes its government to be illegitimate, unresponsive, and oppressive even to those not inclined to revolutionary activity. Small terrorist bands can exist for many years underground in even technologically sophisticated countries like Germany, but they cannot grow because the general population supports the status quo. On the other hand, terrorism can develop into a revolutionary movement in a society where wide sectors of the population are disaffected and therefore will give aid and support to illegal anti government activities. The state will be successful in suppressing such activities but only at the cost of extreme brutality: imprisonment, torture, disappearances, and murder.

One of the rational reasons for terrorism is that counterterrorism security measures can eventually become so costly that a government, for example in a colonial setting, prefers withdrawal to continued occupation. Indiscriminate terrorist acts (targeting random civilians, as in the bombing of a cafeteria) are more disruptive and costly since security forces, not knowing where the terrorists will strike next, need to be spread more thinly. This tactic also keeps the general population on edge and disrupts the normal flow of commerce and leisure activity. Although it may not demoralize the general population, it will frighten some people sufficiently that they will emigrate. There is now apparently a net outflow of population from Israel, for example. Similarly, as casualties due to terrorist attacks mounted during the Algerian war of independence in the 1950s, colonists began to reevaluate their futures, and some debarked for mainland France.

Terrorism is not infrequently motivated primarily by the calculation that it will provoke counterterror actions in which innocent people are victimized (by random house searches, arrests, beatings, or even the bulldozing of houses believed to have sheltered terrorists or their supporters, a tactic used by the Israeli military against Palestinians suspected of terrorism, or of sheltering terrorists, or even just relatives of terrorists). Such tactics create sympathy and generate recruits from among the victims for the terrorists' or the rebels' cause. Carefully targeted assassinations or sabotage, sometimes intended more to raise political awareness within a subjugated population than to disrupt the normal functioning of the society, can also provoke overreaction by the state, generating still more adherents to the cause.

What kinds of people engage in terrorism? What kinds of people are prepared to sacrifice their own lives, not just in general but specifically as suicide bombers who attack innocent civilians or target specific individuals such as soldiers or police? The media paint them as cowards for attacking the innocent, usually without warning. Yet this is an evasion, for clearly they would not be effective as terrorists, or assassins, if they warned their victims (in contrast to saboteurs who issue warnings so as to avoid unnecessary bloodshed). Who are the cowards, those who are prepared to sacrifice their lives for a cause, or those who drop bombs on cities filled with civilians from such high altitudes that they are unlikely to be hit by anti-aircraft fire?

It is often assumed that poverty breeds terrorists (or radicals more generally). Individuals who become active in radical or extremist causes are often motivated to do so because they identify with a population that is poor, oppressed, and exploited. Typically, however, it is not the poor themselves who become activists, at least at first, it is intellectuals, students, and professionals, those who are impelled by what they see rather than what they personally experience. They are angered and frustrated by conditions that affect their co-nationals, co-religionists, or more generally the subordinate population of a country. These conditions can include racial discrimination as well. Almost by definition, such people have been exposed to wider experiences, ideas, and travel. They may have seen what other movements have accomplished. They have been able to compare the misery of their people to the superior conditions of others. Many terrorists, including suicide bombers, are or were members of well-to-do families, and better educated than most of their conationals. This observation is borne out when we examine the biographies of terrorists, including suicide bombers, but also of assassins, and more generally the leading activists of many kinds of revolutionary movements. Ernesto "Che" Guevara is probably one of the best-known examples.

The spotlight of public attention has logically been on the issue of suicide bombers ever since the attacks on the World Trade Center and the Pentagon in September 2001. There is actually a long history of suicide for a cause. Most Americans old enough to remember World War II will recall the Japanese kamikaze pilots who, toward the very end of the war, attempted to fly their small fighter planes into American warships in order to damage or destroy them, sometimes successfully.

A number of studies have completely undermined the thesis that terrorists, and more specifically suicide bombers, are socially marginal, isolated, frustrated, depressed, or friendless people. Scott Atran, a researcher at the National Center for Scientific Research in Paris, mentions interviews with 250 Palestinian suicide volunteers and their recruiters. "They all seemed to be entirely normal members of their families" (the *New York Times*, May 5, 2003). Robert A. Pape, a political scientist at the University of Chicago, compiled a list of 188 suicide bombings from 1980 to 2001, and found little evidence even that fanatical adherence to fundamentalist religion was much of a factor. He reports that "what nearly all suicide terrorist campaigns have in common is a specific secular and strategic goal: to compel liberal democracies to withdraw military forces from territory that the terrorists consider to be their homeland" (the *New York Times*, September 22, 2003). Even Osama bin Laden's initial objective was the withdrawal of U.S. military forces from Islamic states in the Persian Gulf.

It makes perfect sense that suicide terrorists are well integrated with their families and their culture, rather than being isolated, lonely individuals on the margins of society. It is this very tight integration that provides a clue to motivation. Emile Durkheim, the great French sociologist, published his groundbreaking study *Le Suicide* in 1897. (The English-language version came out in 1951.) In this work, which is considered by many sociologists to be the very first to use modern statistical methods in the study of a social problem, Durkheim describes several types of suicide, one of which he calls *altruistic*. This includes suicides of men who fail to die in battle and become old and sick, women on their husbands' death, and followers or servants on the deaths of their chiefs. Durkheim noted that such individuals are very highly integrated into societies that are extremely cohesive. Their suicides are normal, and obligatory. Less obligatory but still part of the social norms are suicides as the aftermath of a defeat or dishonor, or even as martyrdom for a religious reason. Although Durkheim does not discuss suicide attacks on others even though there were numerous instances of suicidal assassinations in his time, the implication of his thesis for contemporary suicide bombers is clear, and is supported by considerable evidence.

If the suicide bomber is perhaps overintegrated into his or her society, are there some societies more inclined to supporting altruistic suicide than others? Even if terrorism is based on a rational calculation, as suggested earlier, are there cultures where suicidal attacks are more acceptable than others? Durkheim believed that altruistic suicide was more common among Hindu, Buddhist, and Jainist religious groups but less so among Jews, Christians, and Muslims because the latter are more individualistically oriented. "In our contemporary societies," he wrote, "as individual personality becomes increasingly free from the collective personality," even martyrdom (as with early Christians) will no longer be prevalent.

A different approach is taken by Willard Gaylin, a psychotherapist and author of *Hatred: The Psychological Descent into Violence*. He believes, with Durkheim, that a society such as Japan, where ritual suicide is "a respectable tradition," is markedly different from the United States, where "suicide is almost invariably viewed as a sign of mental illness." There are cultural differences between societies and we must be careful, he says, about making moral judgments that place one society on a higher plane than the other. On the other hand, he continues, "some cultures are morally corrupt." He calls them "cultures of hatred," and he argues that Palestinians have become such a culture, while Israelis have not. The difference is twofold. First, "Palestinians daily demonstrate . . . their delight at the sight of the macerated victims of suicide bombers, and their pride in the bombers," while Israelis, "even when they have clearly committed atrocities, have struggled with shame . . . not self-congratulation." Second, radical Islam (as distinct from Islam in general) is in the business of creating hatred and, like other fundamentalist religions, promotes passionate belief. This is the context, he implies, in which suicide bombers can be recruited and will be supported by the community.

How valid is this cultural approach? Durkheim's research (and that of many others) makes a good case that there are cultural and historical differences among societies (including religious differences) such that suicide is more common in some than in others. The same is true specifically for altruistic suicide. Although Durkheim does not discuss suicidal attacks, Dr. Gaylin is probably right that the overwhelming majority of North Americans see it as an aberration even as sacrificing one's life for one's comrades on the battlefront is a noble act. On the other hand, the data do not support Gaylin's thesis that fundamentalist Islam is particularly culpable, as we have noted earlier. Robert A. Pape points out, for example, that the group that leads in the actual number of suicidal incidents he examined (prior to September 2001) were the Tamil Tigers, who are Hindu in background but thoroughly secular. Nor were the 9/11 terrorists particularly religious. Many of the group were improbable suspects under any of the prevailing theories. The conclusion is that there is no single terrorist profile—except a hard dedication to a cause.

· 7 ·

Fighting Back:
Dealing with Being One-Down

$\mathcal{I}$n the years immediately following World War II, the situation facing African-Americans, particularly in the South, continued to be one of separate and unequal. As the U.S. Civil Rights Commission's 1961 Report delicately put it, "In some 100 counties in eight Southern states there is reason to believe that Negro citizens are prevented—by outright discrimination or by fear of physical violence or economic reprisal—from exercising the right to vote. . . . there are many counties in the South where a substantial Negro population not only has no voice in government, but suffers extensive deprivation—legal, economic, educational, and social." Efforts to change this picture were resisted vigorously. The white South reacted against the U.S. Supreme Court's 1954 school desegregation decision with massive resistance, often led by the White Citizens' Councils, white supremacist organizations closely linked to the KKK At its peak around 1956 the Citizens' Council movement claimed 250,000 members. (Some of its remnants are affiliated with some of the extremist organizations discussed in chapter 5.)

In the Deep Southern states (South Carolina, Georgia, Alabama, Mississippi, and Louisiana) less than 500,000 African-Americans were registered to vote in 1958. Mississippi had seven counties from 60 to 72 percent African-American in population, in which not one of them was registered. In the rural areas particularly, fear of racist terror, whether in the form of night riders or mobs, kept blacks "in their place." This fear, it could logically be argued, was the other side of the coin of white fear: access to the ballot in such areas implied a political revolution since blacks constituted majorities. It would mean black sheriffs, mayors, police chiefs, and other power-holding positions. It would mean a collapse of the Old Order. Small wonder that reform was resisted.

But the South had been changing. By 1950 nearly half the African-American population lived in cities. A middle class of black businesspeople and professionals was growing. The segregated black colleges became breeding grounds for intellectual ferment and potential protests. In December 1955 the Montgomery Bus Boycott, led by Reverend Martin Luther King Jr., was launched. This was the context in which the next major step in the civil rights movement was to take place. The African-American population looked at its one-down position, the prejudice, discrimination, violence, and frequently hatred that it faced, and, not for the first time by any means, was fighting back.

On February 1, 1960, four black male students at North Carolina Agricultural and Technical College went into the F. W. Woolworth store in downtown Greensboro and sat down at the lunch counter to wait for service. Blacks had never been served there, and that day was no exception. But the next day the students returned with some friends, and the day after, and after. Word of this nonviolent action quickly spread, and within ten days there were lunch counter sit-ins in Durham, Charlotte, and Raleigh, and within sixty days sit-ins and other nonviolent direct action had spread to places as far removed as Xenia, Ohio, and Sarasota, Florida. One year later the Congress of Racial Equality, a pioneer in developing nonviolent tactics and training in the field of civil rights, announced that 138 communities (mainly in the Upper South) had desegregated at least some facilities. At that point, however, little progress had been made in the Deep South, where resistance to reform was fiercest. In Orangeburg, South Carolina, 388 black college students were arrested, put into a stockade, and sprayed with water in freezing weather. Elsewhere hundreds of students were gassed, attacked by police dogs, had burning cigars or ammonia thrown on them at lunch counters, or were beaten. Eventually some 50,000 students, from both North and South, participated in the sit-in movement directly, or as supporters by picketing Northern outlets of chain stores that were still segregated in Southern communities. Many of them later became leaders in the student left and anti-Vietnam war movements.

Gordon Allport, whose book *The Nature of Prejudice* was published six years before the sit-in movement began, told us that militancy is one of several normal responses to victimization. "In psychological parlance," he said, "frustration breeds aggression." This is an extremely important observation. It is the key to understanding not only militant "fighting back," but a set of other behaviors by one-down individuals and groups, ranging from intrafamilial assault, rape, and homicide to drug use and nonaltruistic suicide to the type of religious practices common among very poor populations. Given this range of behaviors, militancy is actually the most positive and progressive of all the strategies available to oppressed groups. But we need to understand some of the other strategies as well because they often constitute phases that coexist, and sometimes lead to, the development of protest movements.

"Perhaps the simplest response a victim can make is to deny his [sic] membership in a disparaged group," Allport wrote. "Passing" as white has historically been quite common among light-skinned African-Americans. Even within a single family, one member may, due to lighter skin, choose to pass as white and perhaps have to cut ties with the family of origin permanently. The cosmetics industry has made fortunes on skin lighteners and hair straighteners to accommodate the desire of many African-Americans to appear lighter, if not actually to pass.

Many members of immigrant ethnic groups have passed by changing their names to "American," that is, English-sounding, names: from Cohen to Collins, Goldstein to Gold or Guild, and so on, so much so that some English names are assumed to be changed from Eastern European names even when that is not true. An interesting Italian example involves the family name Pietroinferno, translated literally to Firestone. Converting to the dominant religion has been a common method used by Jews, but sometimes also by Catholics, to break through occupational and educational obstacles in many countries. Karl Marx's father, for example, had converted to Lutheranism, and Marx did not identify himself as Jewish. The price for this form of passing has often been ostracism by the family of origin. Intermarriage of Jews to Christians has also carried that price with it, more so in the past than in recent years. Conversion and intermarriage were widely seen as treason in the fight of a persecuted group for its survival.

Some sociologists have argued that as an ethnic group becomes socially more like the dominant group, and economically more successful, its ethnic identification declines. This process increases the likelihood of intermarriage with other ethnic groups, not necessarily even the dominant one, so that identification with the original immigrant group declines further. The typical white Rutgers University student from northern New Jersey does not have four grandparents of the same ethnicity, does not identify with the ethnicity associated with her or his surname, is uninformed about the history of that group or the country from which it came, and in addition does not think this is of any importance. It is well known that for immigrant groups the language of ethnic origin pretty much disappears by the third generation: The first generation speaks, reads, and writes (if it is literate); the second only speaks; the third only understands but does not speak, and then it's over.

The quest for assimilation sometimes goes to extremes. The minority group, in order to be accepted, joins the oppressor group in its antipathy toward other minority groups. It identifies with the oppressor. It becomes as prejudiced toward others as the dominant group. And some of its members lean over backward to try to fit in with the prejudiced attitudes of the dominant group, going so far as to be willing to make jokes demeaning not only other groups, but even their own group. Given that there are class and national differences within the minority group, some members of the upper strata of the minority will demean those of the lower. As Gordon Allport reports, "Lace Curtain" Irish look down on "shanty Irish," just as German Jews look down on Eastern European "ghetto" Jews. In the same way, lighter-skinned African-Americans sometimes look down on their darker-skinned brethren, and African-Caribbeans think themselves superior to North American blacks. This is done in order to try to evade the stereotypes of the minority group that are prevalent in the general public: "we are not like those people, we are different, we are like you."

One form that assimilationism takes is the attempt to prove to the dominant group the worthiness of the victim group by demonstrating the group's loyalty, patriotism, and general adherence to the values of the dominant group, that is, the nation in which the subordinate group finds itself as "guest." The demands of gays for full membership in the armed services, of women to serve in combat units, or the volunteering of Japanese-Americans to fight in World War II are examples of this.

In the early 1930s, when the Nazi movement's attacks on Jews in Germany began to take a more virulent form, one of their propaganda messages was that the Jews had been slackers during World War I. Most Jews in Germany at the time believed in assimilation because they had achieved full rights as German citizens. To counter the Nazi libel, the Jewish war veterans organization went to the trouble of compiling a book listing every single Jewish soldier who had been killed in the war fighting for the Kaiser (a higher proportion, it turned out, than in the general population). In the end, this attempt to prove the Jews' loyalty was useless. Those German Jews who continued to insist that they were Germans first, Jews second, and voluntarily stayed in Germany in the belief that this reasoning would prevail, went to concentration camps and many if not most were killed. Thanks to their Iron Crosses, medals won in combat during World War I, some Jewish veterans survived because they were not sent to death camps.

The quest for assimilation, or if not assimilation then at least equal rights as citizens, is a permanent component of the political agenda of all minority groups. This quest often takes the form of organizing pressure groups to lobby, take legal action to obtain equal rights, run political candidates to promote the interests of the group, or engage in social protest actions such as organizing boycotts against discriminating institutions, or sit–ins (as in the Greensboro example in 1960), to mention just a few tactics. Virtually all disadvantaged and victimized groups, whether racial, religious, gender-based, sexual preference-based, disability-based, or others, engage in social movements that advocate equal rights. These are the movements we call integrationist. The desire peaceably to join the mainstream of society is an eternal dream, to paraphrase Martin Luther King Jr.

While assimilation implies a blending in (and a disappearance of ethnicity), integrationism is more concerned with equal rights than with assimilating. Most organizations and movements dedicated to civil rights are integrationist rather than assimilationist even though assimilation may be the implicit goal in the very long term. If integration is successful, can assimilation be far behind?

Among integrationists there are more moderate, and more radical elements. The moderates concentrate on conventional politics, including lobbying, legislative reform, and court decisions. The National Association for the Advancement of Colored People (NAACP) and the National Organization for Women (NOW) are typical of this tendency. The more radical wing is more prone to direct action: boycotts, sit-ins, and strikes. At the extreme of the radical wing are the more traditional leftists, socialists, and communists, who believe wholeheartedly in the long-term goal of integration ("black and white, unite and fight") but are more inclined to concentrate their organizing efforts on labor unions, farmer protests, poor people's movements, and other class or economic (rather than ethnic, racial, or gender) issues in order to bring people together regardless of their differences for the purpose of creating a better society in which discrimination will hopefully be eliminated. Very often the assumption is that the victimization of minorities is an inherent component of the workings of the current capitalist economic system, so that ultimately only its abolition will succeed in the elimination of the persecution, discrimination, and subordination of minorities of whatever kind.

As we argued in chapter 4, no minority group has ever achieved equal access to the kinds of resources available to the dominant group, even under conditions far more benign than those faced by Jews in Germany, or African-Americans in the segregated South, or any people under colonial rule. It has nevertheless been the case that assimilation has been the goal of most ethnic minority groups in the United States, and most groups, insofar as they have succeeded in joining the mainstream of the society, have lost much of their ethnicity in the process. But not always: As Stephen Steinberg points out in *The Ethnic Myth*, "ethnicity has been preserved most authentically by those groups who, for one reason or another, have remained economically marginal. Even among groups that have experienced wide-scale mobility, the lower-class strata continue to function as a cultural anchor for their more affluent relatives."

What happens when it becomes apparent to significant numbers of victimized groups that the integrationist route is not working out, whether it is because of economic circumstances, political persecution, or the persistence of prejudice and discrimination by the wider population or the state? It is under these conditions that the group remains cohesive, or becomes even more conscious of its identity (racial, religious, or ethnic) and the integrationist message becomes discredited.

Alongside every integrationist movement there arises a second stream that can be described as autonomist or separatist. Sometimes the term nationalist is used. Without exception all oppressed minorities develop both integrationist and autonomist movements, varying only in their relative strengths depending on what country or time period we are examining. This is also true for movements of colonial peoples. Movements for national independence or short of that various forms of political autonomy take place only when colonial people come to the realization that the colonial power will not grant equal rights and will not allow integration of the subject population into the institutions of power that it controls.

A common pattern of behavior for members of one-down minority groups as they cope with a situation that denies them entry into the dominant society is to emphasize the symbols of identity that differentiate the group from its oppressors. This can take the form of searching for the historical roots of the group and adopting cultural items associated with those roots, including cuisine. In the late 1960s and during the 1970s it was common on college campuses to see African-Americans with "Afro" hairstyles and West African items of clothing. There was a sudden interest in studying African languages such as Hausa and KiSwahili, as well as Arabic. African history became a more popular subject area. Similarly there has been a small religious revival among Jewish students and (even among secular Jews) renewed interest in the Yiddish language and its literature. "Chicano studies" programs were introduced in many Western and Southwestern universities. The sale of cultural artifacts such as ethnic clothing, musical recordings, religious objects, and works of art became, and remains, a minor industry. This can clearly be seen in any predominantly minority neighborhood, whether African-American, Jewish, Mexican-American (or Latin American more generally), or Caribbean, of any large city not to mention the neighborhoods of more recent immigrant groups from Eastern Europe. Among all cultural items, cuisine associated with an ethnicity seems to be the most lasting mark of identity, even as the wider society adopts and adapts culinary items, blending them into the mainstream. But these "culturalist" phenomena are political only in the most superficial sense. And they are co-optable because they are commercial products, subject to all the usual rules of capitalist economics. Insofar as they prove to be commercially successful products they become targets to be annexed to the market institutions that are controlled by the dominant groups in society. This is not much of a contribution to the development of an autonomist political movement.

Autonomist movements have in common the demand that the particular group, be it a "ghettoized" minority within a larger society or a nationality living under colonial rule, should be self-determining when it comes to decisions over its economic structure, cultural institutions, and political or governing mechanisms. The other commonality is the conviction that continuing to live under the domination of another group must end, and that attempts to integrate, or achieve equal rights as citizens, are futile. The sentiment among autonomists is that the idea that "they" will ever let "us" have equal access to resources is a delusion because of the depth of prejudice and hatred of the subordinate group by the dominant one. Even more important perhaps is the conviction that the dominant group has clear vested interests in maintaining the status quo, or indeed worsening the degree of persecution and oppression.

But there are a number of very different approaches to this broad agenda. In chapter 4 we saw that many countries contain within their often artificial boundaries national minorities differing in language, religion, history, economic circumstances, and sometimes race (or physical appearance) from the larger nation in which they find themselves. Following the collapse of the Soviet Union and Yugoslavia in the early 1990s, these subgroups raised the banner of national self-determination and in some cases attempted to delink politically from the larger nation. This was frequently opposed by the central government intent on maintaining a cohesive political structure. The result in a few cases was military insurgency, and in others a perpetual state of tension between the national minority and the central government. In the worst case, in the former Yugoslavia, extended insurgencies and outright warfare between the former component nationalities ensued, with massive civilian and military casualties, pogroms, large-scale expulsions of populations, vast numbers living in refugee camps, and the like. This is not over. In the Caucasus area of the former Soviet Union more than two dozen different "ethnolinguistic" groups coexist, but not very peacefully. An insurgent movement in Chechnya continues to battle Russia, and has taken the war to the heartland in the form of terrorist attacks. Wars over territory among the smaller nationalities also continue. All these movements for national independence see themselves as oppressed, and often conceptualize this oppression as colonialism. Each is organized around a common denominator of culture: a unique and different history, language, and/or religion forms a core of national identity that becomes the rallying point for the struggle.

This ethnocentrism or focusing on one's own ethnicity as central to one's identity can, and frequently does, go to the extreme of claiming cultural or even racial superiority over other groups. "You are better than the white man," Malcolm X said in one of his street corner speeches in Harlem in the early 1960s. "To be prejudiced *in favor* of one's own kind is a natural reflex of outgroup prejudice against one's kind," Allport wrote.

Ethnocentrism is frequently linked to nationalism, which is when the people of a nation put their national identity at the center of their consciousness. This sometimes develops into superpatriotism, or what we call flag-waving.

Nationalism and nationalist movements often promote a sense of superiority. There is only a short step from superiority to supremacism. Supremacism whether white, black, religious, or national implies prejudiced attitudes and beliefs about the "inferior" other and is used to justify their mistreatment. When whole countries are taken over by nationalist fervor, as in wartime, supremacism can result in the mistreatment, expulsion, and even extermination of minority groups. In warfare it is a rare nation that does not negatively stereotype the external enemy as well as internal minorities that are believed to be disloyal.

"Black nationalism," one form of autonomist movement within the African-American community, proceeds on the assumption that African-Americans constitute a nation that is subject to colonial rule within the United States. They are a nation in the sense that they have a specific history going back to Africa and slavery, and that this history has created a certain ethnic culture that differentiates it from the dominant society. The term "black nationalism," however, is commonly used as an umbrella term for many kinds of African-American identity-based movements.

Another autonomist tendency is the idea of maintaining or creating separate economic and cultural institutions short of actual nationhoods. The role of the African-American church, which was born during slavery and segregation, in sustaining the black community is well known. But some religious groups, including the Nation of Islam and, in earlier days, the church led by Father Divine, not to mention the black nationalist movement led by Marcus Garvey among others, also advocated and promoted black small businesses as one avenue toward the self-determination of black communities. From time to time there have also been black political parties. These have not, however, had any success given a political structure that makes it so difficult for third parties in general. Most African-Americans have voted for the Democratic Party, at least at the national level, since the time of Franklin D. Roosevelt and the New Deal.

A very old form of autonomism involves the demand by some African-Americans for a piece of territory, a state or two that would become a black nation. In the late 1920s the Communist Party briefly called for a Soviet-style Republic in the "Black Belt" of the South, the old plantation areas where blacks constituted majorities. This approach had little following since most African-Americans then and now favor the integrationist route. The situation is different for Native-Americans, the peoples Canadians call "First Nations," since they already live in contiguous territories. And in Puerto Rico there is a long history of a movement that seeks complete independence from the United States A political party dedicated to that goal exists even now, though it no longer has the appeal of earlier years.

African-Americans have logically felt some sense of identification with Africa and with the specific West African countries whence their ancestors came to the Western Hemisphere as slaves. The idea that all Africans, regardless of location, constitute a single people or nation and that there should be a movement promoting a supranational political entity in which all Africans might find a home is called Pan-Africanism. Numerous prominent African-Americans have involved themselves in this quest, including WEB DuBois. The *Manifesto of the Second Pan-African Congress* of 1921, which he wrote, concluded that all of Africa would either be absorbed into two or three of the larger non-African countries, with full equality for blacks, or Africa would see "the rise of a great black African state founded in Peace and Good Will." (The *Manifesto* is included in Bracey, Meier, and Rudwick's anthology *Black Nationalism in America*.)

Another kind of autonomist movement is the "zionistic" type. It is logical that when a people believes it has no future within a country it will look for another place, a refuge or homeland outside. Both separatist and zionistic tendencies among African-Americans go back to before the Civil War. There were a number of "colonization" schemes that aimed at transporting at least some African-Americans back to Africa. But by far the largest of these endeavors took the form of the Universal Negro Improvement Association, which was founded by a charismatic Jamaican, Marcus Garvey, in 1914. Garvey, nicknamed "the Black Moses," advocated that American blacks return to their homeland, Africa (specifically Liberia), and organized a steamship line for that purpose. He emphasized pride in the race, and dressed himself and his followers in military-style uniforms. The integrationists of the NAACP deplored him, and in turn he had utter contempt for them. Eventually he ran afoul of the federal government and went to prison. President Calvin Coolidge pardoned him after two years in the Atlanta Penitentiary and he was deported. In terms of numbers of adherents the Garvey movement was probably the largest protest movement in African-American history. Nor did the movement die with Garvey's own ill fortune, for many of his adherents went on to play important roles in other protest movements. Some of the early figures of what was to become the Nation of Islam had had Garveyite ties.

Within the Jewish population Zionism is the tendency that similarly advocates a return to a homeland. "The longing of the Jewish people for the return to the land of its past is as old as the diaspora," wrote Alex Bein, author of the standard biography of modern Zionism's founder, Theodore Herzl. Herzl, born in Budapest in the Austro-Hungarian Empire, organized the first Zionist Congress in Basel, Switzerland, in 1897. Later the political influence of Zionism would culminate in the creation of the State of Israel out of the British Mandate of Palestine, which had been carved from the territory of the defeated Ottoman Empire after World War I. Among American Jews today, it is safe to say, sympathy for the Zionist idea of a Jewish homeland in Israel, short of actually emigrating, is the dominant political tendency. But it is not the only tendency, nor was it prior to World War II. Among German Jews, integrationism was dominant. Among the Jews of Eastern Europe, especially within the more secular segments of the Jewish working class, a Jewish socialist movement called the Bund thrived alongside and in opposition to Zionism. Its thesis was that a socialist transformation would solve the Jews' problem of prejudice and discrimination, and it collaborated with other socialist movements while at the same time attempting to maintain a Jewish cultural identity. Not quite integrationist, it nevertheless believed Zionism to be the wrong strategy, just as African-American socialists such as DuBois and A. Philip Randolph deplored the Garveyite prescription. Garvey and Herzl, although very different personalities, can be seen as symbolic of the zionistic alternative within the broad range of possible social movements among oppressed ethnic or racial minorities.

Autonomist movements come in many forms just as integrationist movements do. But there is a deeper division within the autonomist family. This is the conflict between "culturalists" and "radicals," or in nationalist movements, between cultural nationalists and radical nationalists. In brief outline, the culturalist program says: 1) All of us are united by our common denominator identity (whether it be race, religion, gender, or nationality). 2) The enemy is the collective "other": white people, Christians, men, the French colonial oppressor population in its entirety. 3) The primary objective is to become autonomous, to get "them" out of our lives, to get them to leave our territory, to get them off our backs. All other objectives are secondary, to be dealt with after the primary objective has been achieved. All other objectives are potentially divisive and need to be suppressed. 4) Consequently, by implication, a great deal of education is not necessary; a set of simple, unifying slogans (for example, "Black Power") will suffice. 5) It is assumed that this unifying, common denominator approach will succeed in attaining wide support. This can be called the "minimalist" strategy.

The radical program says the opposite: 1) We are not all united, because some of us are linked, by political or economic interests, to the dominant power. 2) The enemy is not the entire "other" because the "other" also contains oppressed people. Therefore it is some of us (and potentially, in the future, some of them) against some of them (and some of us who work in their service). The line is one of class, in that "we" are generally workers, peasants, and others of the lower strata, and "they" are the economically better off, the bourgeoisie, but also their servants such as the police (most colonial powers recruit police forces from the local population). 3) The primary objective, to become autonomous, is coupled with a program of what society should look like afterward. This program, for radicals, implies if it does not say so specifically, some form of socialistic society with more self-determination for workers and more rights for the lower strata in general. Conversely, this implies some restrictions on private enterprise. This program is divisive, and therefore 4) an extensive educational effort must be mounted in order to obtain wide support. 5) It is assumed that even in the short run the culturalist approach will not attain wide support because many people will question why they should fight to rid themselves of one (foreign, "other") oppressor only to end up with another (our own native oppressor). Only a radical approach that promises to end all oppression will succeed in attracting the mass following necessary to win. This can be called the "maximalist" strategy.

This debate is reflected within virtually all autonomist movements. In the Algerian war of independence against France, two liberation movements contested for dominance—the FLN, which ultimately won out, called for a movement that muted class differences, while the MNA, which lost, advocated an explicitly socialist program. The war between them took violent form, involving assassinations and battles between rival guerrilla military units. In the Spanish Civil War a similar conflict within the Loyalist (republican) side took place, with Communists and Socialists opting for a minimal program of defeating Franco while other leftists and anarchists advocated a more radical anti-capitalist program as part of the anti-fascist struggle. Here too blood was shed. Within the Zionist camp, aside from the conflict with the socialist Bundists, there was, for a long time, a debate between more conservative Zionists and those advocating a more labor and socialist program, and even collaboration with Palestinian nationalists.

In the late 1960s a literally murderous conflict broke out between cultural nationalists and radical nationalists in the African-American community. An organization called US (United Slaves) promoted a primarily culturalist message, while the Black Panther Party organized around a more socialist, class-oriented program.

In the feminist movement the more radical elements outside the mainstream integrationist camp are themselves divided between self-styled radical feminists who emphasize the unity of all women against the main enemy, the institution of patriarchy, and socialist feminists who identify the main enemy as capitalism, with patriarchy as an outgrowth of it (as described long ago in *The Communist Manifesto*). In this case the radicals are closer to culturalism.

Within the current Palestinian women's movement, one camp, which would correspond to Palestinian cultural nationalism, proposes to postpone the struggle for women's rights until after national independence, while the other says the two struggles should be parallel. Other Palestinian nationalist organizations are also divided between those oriented to a more cultural nationalist program and more radical elements.

In all of these movements the most important issue is whether or not more radical programs (socialism, labor rights, land reform, gay and lesbian rights, women's rights, peace, and so on) should be incorporated into the basic autonomist or nationalist demand (independence, typically, for anti-colonialist movements). The same issue divides the integrationist camp as well, for many integrationist movements are reluctant to have other issues intrude on the main one. It has been very difficult, for example, for lesbians to get a hearing within the wider integrationist women's movement. In the civil rights movement of the 1960s, as Martin Luther King Jr. began to criticize the Vietnam War and orient more to the issues facing not just African-Americans but all poor people, mainstream civil rights leaders started to distance themselves from him. This debate was cut short by his assassination in 1968.

At what point does a victimized, oppressed people (or one that perceives itself as such—not necessarily the same thing, but with many of the same consequences) move beyond the personal? At what point does the aggression part of the frustration-aggression thesis surmount the kinds of in-group aggression (homicide, assault, drugs) characteristic of many oppressed populations described so well by Fanon? When do people go beyond "passing," identifying with the oppressor, "fitting in," and the like? When does aggression become outwardly directed to take a political rather than a criminal form? When do protest movements of whatever kind (not all movements are positive) become an acceptable and desirable strategy?

A number of necessary if not sufficient conditions seem to be present for a social movement to begin to take off. Sociologists have pointed to the idea of "relative deprivation" as one factor. Many if not most people, especially in the Third World, have been deprived for a very long time yet have not protested because they believed their lot was inevitable. Once, however, they come in contact with some other population with which they can compare themselves, they can see that things can be different. African-Americans could always readily see others who were better off and freer. After World War II, as more and more African countries rid themselves of colonialism the question "why not us, too?" inevitably came up.

In preliterate societies in the South Pacific that had been victimized by colonialism (native cultures were torn apart when European colonialists forced men into virtual slavery on plantations), what anthropologists call "revitalization movements" ensued as natives came into contact with the world outside their villages. During World War II when some natives saw people who looked like them (African-American soldiers) and were clearly better off with access to vast quantities of material goods, a new wave of these movements took place. Some of these developed into movements for independence from Great Britain.

The development of a movement also requires a sense of group identity, of "we-ness." Whether it is based on nationality, religion, language, gender, race, or class, consciousness of belonging to an oppressed group (rather than merely being individually victimized) is essential. This consciousness is heightened by an awareness of the history of the group, including its history of presumed past glories and past protests or uprisings. It does not matter that this history is sometimes exaggerated or even invented. For example, it has proven impossible to organize exploited workers to change their lot (via unions or parties) unless there is what Marxists call class consciousness, the awareness that they are members of a larger community of the working class, and identify with that class.

A third precondition for the rise of movements is what can roughly be termed "historical ripeness." This is hard to pin down because if a movement develops, it is obvious that conditions were ripe, and if it does not, then clearly they were not, but this doesn't get us far in analyzing just what ripeness or readiness means. One factor that plays a role is a political and economic environment in which the established way of doing things, including the generally accepted ideology, the prevailing economic rules, and possibly the way government operates, has become discredited. Often elements of the ruling group begin to defect, that is dissent and join oppositional groups and incipient movements. Another factor that is often present is that some reforms have already been accomplished for whatever historical reason so that hope for further changes has become realistic. At the same time, an alternative ideology or vision of what a better future might look like is articulated and begins to gain a following.

This ideology, or message, has to make sense to a large number of people. It has to have an appeal. And it helps to have a charismatic messenger deliver this new way of looking at life. The quality called *charisma* (from the Greek, meaning to have a gift, to be the favored one) is easier to understand by identifying people who have it or had it than to define it more specifically. It is not a quality that is limited to good people or bad: Martin Luther King Jr., Malcolm X, Garvey, Hitler, Mussolini, Trotsky, Eugene V. Debs readily come to mind. It is the charismatic leader who understands what the message needs to be, and how to get it across, for better or worse.

Clearly some movements are retrogressive with respect to human rights and the amelioration of discriminatory conditions for victimized, oppressed groups. They present alternatives that can be quite popular, as we saw in chapter 5. Demagogues manipulate fear and promote xenophobia. They promote conspiracy theories and scapegoat whatever targets are convenient: Jews, immigrants, other minorities. They propose false solutions to real problems, and target the wrong sources of these problems. They often have wealthy backers with an interest in maintaining the status quo. They have sometimes opened the way to totalitarian states.

Given that all social movements have certain characteristics in common, and that some have resulted in totalitarianism, a number of social thinkers have proposed that all movements involving masses of people are vulnerable to manipulation by demagogues and have totalitarian potential, and therefore should be opposed. But this view would paralyze victimized groups. There would be no way forward except the goodwill of dominant groups, a perspective that seems naïve at best. This view must be rejected because many if not most movements do not, in fact, lead to totalitarianism.

Most of the movements discussed in this chapter fall into the broad category of "progressive," although an argument can be made that cultural nationalism has many retrogressive aspects and in the long run will have more negative than positive results. Progressive or left-oriented movements are those that create more possibilities for the development of human potential, are structured more democratically (rather than top-down authoritarian), and have as their targets the real sources of social problems rather than scapegoats. They generally advocate economic redistributive policies. They oppose all forms of discrimination based on characteristics such as race, gender, religion, or national background. Despite their flaws (and no movement is perfect) their outcomes have been positive. Many examples come to mind: the social democratic and labor movements of Western Europe, the Socialist Party of Eugene Debs's day, the nonviolent civil rights movement of the United States, the integrationist women's movements around the world, the Polish Solidarity movement in the 1980s, many segments of the global justice movement today, many labor union struggles in the United States and elsewhere, and many (though by no means all) anti-colonial national independence movements.

Not all movements succeed. Many progressive movements have been defeated in part, if not entirely. Totalitarian states have suppressed many democratic movements so successfully that it has taken many years for their populations once again to develop democratic structures after those states passed from the scene. Yet resistance to oppression seems to be as much a part of human nature as any of the more selfish attributes that some social scientists seem to emphasize, if not more.

A quandary was implied at the end of the prologue. How are we to move ordinary men (and women) from being willing executioners (or haters, or oppressors) in the direction of developing nonauthoritarian, democratic ways of coping with their problems? How are victimized and oppressed groups to find a progressive, positive way forward toward greater freedom? It can only be through becoming committed to working in movements for social change that are democratic in structure, humanitarian in spirit, and dedicated, one step at a time or more, to the abolition of oppressive social and economic relations.

References

Adorno, Theodor W., et al. *The Authoritarian Personality*. Harper and Brothers, 1950.

Aho, James A. *The Politics of Righteousness: Idaho Christian Patriotism*. Washington University Press, 1990. Also *This Thing of Darkness: A Sociology of the Enemy*. Washington University Press, 1994.

Allport, Gordon. *The Nature of Prejudice*. Doubleday, 1958 (orig. 1954).

Athens, Lonnie. *The Creation of Dangerous Violent Criminals*. Routledge, 1989.

Beck, Aaron. *Prisoners of Hate*. Perennial/HarperCollins Publishers, 1999.

Bein, Alex. *Theodore Herzl, A Biography*. Jewish Publication Society of America, 1940.

Berlet, Chip. "Hard Times on the Hard Right." *The Public Eye,* Spring 2002. Also *Eyes Right!* South End Press, 1995.

Bracey, John H. Jr., August Meier, and Elliott Rudwick, eds. *Black Nationalism in America*. Bobbs-Merrill, 1970.

Bronner, Stephen Eric. *A Rumor About the Jews*. St. Martin's Press, 2000.

Brown, Norman O. *Love's Body*. University of California Press, 1967.

Brown, Richard Maxwell. "The History of Extralegal Violence in Support of Community Values," in Thomas Rose (ed.), *Violence in America*. Random House/Vintage, 1969.

Browning, Christopher R. *Ordinary Men: Reserve Police Battalion 101 and the Final Solution in Poland*. HarperPerennial, 1998.

Cleaver, Eldridge. *Soul on Ice*. Delta Publishing Company, 1968.

Cox, Oliver C. *Caste, Class and Race*. Monthly Review Press, 1970. Orig. Doubleday, 1948.

Davis, Mike. *Magical Urbanism: Latinos Reinvent the U.S. City*. Verso, 2000.

Dollard, John. *Caste and Class in a Southern Town*. Doubleday, 1957. Orig. Yale University.

Domhoff, G. William. *Who Rules America?* McGraw-Hill, 2002.

Durkheim, Emile. *Suicide*. Free Press (Macmillan), 1951. Orig. 1897.

Ellis, John. *The Social History of the Machine Gun*. Johns Hopkins University Press, 1986.

Ezekiel, Ralph. *The Racist Mind: Portraits of American Neo-Nazis and Klansmen*. Viking, 1995.

Fanon, Frantz. *The Wretched of the Earth*. Grove Press, 1963.

Gaylin, Willard. *Hatred*. Public Affairs/Perseus, 2003.

Grier, William H., and Price M. Cobb. *Black Rage*. Basic Books, 1968.

Herrnstein, Richard J., and Charles Murray. *The Bell Curve*. Free Press, 1994.

Hofstadter, Richard. *The Paranoid Style in American Politics and Other Essays*. Random House/Vintage, 1967. Orig. 1952.

Kardiner, Abram, and Lionel Ovesey. *The Mark of Oppression*. Norton, 1951.

Kogon, Eugen. *The Theory and Practice of Hell*. Berkley Publishing Group, 1998.

Lee, Alfred McClung. *Terrorism in Northern Ireland*. General Hall, 1983.

Levin, Jack, and Jack McDevitt. *Hate Crimes*. Plenum Press, 1993.

Lipset, Seymour Martin. *Political Man*. Johns Hopkins University Press, 1981. Orig. 1959.

Lummis, C. Douglas. "Concerning a Small Matter of Definition," *New Politics* X (1) (Summer 2004).

Marable, Manning. *How Capitalism Underdeveloped Black America*. South End Press, 2000.

Marcuse, Herbert. *One-Dimensional Man*. Beacon Press, 1964.

Memmi, Albert. *Dominated Man*. Beacon Press, 1969.

Millet, Kate. *Sexual Politics*. University of Illinois Press, 2000 reprint. Orig. 1970.

Morris, Aldon. *Origins of the Civil Rights Movement*. Free Press, 1986.

Myrdal, Gunnar. *An American Dilemma*. Harper and Brothers, 1944.

Omi, Michael, and Howard Winant. *Racial Formation in the United States*, 2nd ed. Routledge, 1994.

Oppenheimer, Martin. *The State in Modern Society*. Humanity Books/ Prometheus, 2000.

Park, Robert E. *Race and Culture*. Free Press, 1950. Orig. 1926.

Paz, Octavio. *The Labyrinth of Solitude*. Grove Press, 1968, 1985.

Piven, Frances Fox, and Richard A. Cloward. *Poor People's Movements*. Random House/Vintage, 1979.

Reich, Wilhelm. *The Mass Psychology of Fascism*. Orgone Institute Press, 1946.

Rummel, R. J. *Death by Government*. Transaction, 1994.

Sennett, Richard, and Jonathan Cobb. *The Hidden Injuries of Class*. Random House/Vintage, 1973.

Steinberg, Stephen. *The Ethnic Myth*. Beacon Press, 1982.

Stiles, T. J. *Jesse James: Last Rebel of the Civil War*. Alfred A. Knopf, 2002.

Trotsky, Leon. "Terrorism in War and Revolution," in *A Trotsky Anthology*. Dell Publishing, 1964. Orig. 1920.

Tucker, William H. *The Politics of Racial Research*. University of Illinois Press, 1994.

U.S. Commission on Civil Rights. *1961 Report, v. 1, Voting*. U.S. Government Printing Office.

Weber, Max. *The Protestant Ethic and the Spirit of Capitalism*. Roxbury, 2002. Orig. 1904–05.

Wilson, William Julius. *When Work Disappears*. Random House/Vintage, 1997.

Winant, Howard. *The World Is a Ghetto*. Basic Books, 2001.

Wright, Richard. *Black Boy*. Harper and Brothers, 1937.

Zweigenhaft, Richard L., and G. William Domhoff. *Diversity in the Power Elite*. Yale University Press, 1998.

Index

aboriginal populations, effects of colonialism on, 43–44

abortion, activism against, 56, 60

Abu Ghraib prison, abuse incident in, 10, 13, 14, 15, 16, 20, 24

abuse: as boundary maintenance, 30; of children, 11; fears of, 18–19, 26; forms of oppression with, 24–37; incidence of, 10; rationalization for, 14, 22. *See also* blaming the victim; dehumanization; I, the Jury; relativization; sanitization; trivialization

acceptance, forms of, 34–36

Adorno, Theodor, 62

African-American populations: black nationalist movements in, 90; civil rights movement in, 83–84; conflict of reform movements in, 93; disadvantages of, 48; education outcomes of, 49, 50; employment levels of, 31–32, 49; as Negro Problem, 47–48; oppression/abuse of, 19, 48; Pan-Africanism in, 91; "passing" of, 85; returning to Africa by, 91; school integration of, 83; stereotypes/myths of, 6, 11; as target of extremist groups, 54, 55, 56, 58;

U.S. demographics of, 45; voting patterns of, 90. *See also* minority populations

aggression: frustration-aggression thesis of, 2, 27; in-group aggression in, 27; theories on human forms of, 3

Aho, James, 57, 61

AIDS, 16, 18

Air America, 65

Algeria, war of independence in, 93

Allen, Woody, 30

Allport, Gordon: on authoritarianism and prejudice, 62; on coping mechanisms, 36; on ethnocentrism, 89; on hatred, 3; on militant protest groups, 84; on minorities being accepted, 35; on "passing," 85; social psychology studies of, 24; on stratification with minority group, 86

Al Qaida, 3

altruistic suicide, 81

Amaru, Tupac, 75

American Civil Liberties Union, 61

An American Dilemma (Myrdal), 47

American Enterprise Institute, 64

Amnesty International, 11

anti-corporatism, 61

Anti-Defamation League (ADL), 54

About the Author

Martin Oppenheimer, professor emeritus of sociology at Rutgers University, has been involved in civil rights, peace, and labor campaigns since his college days. He is the author of several books and articles in these areas, including *The Sit-In Movement of 1960, The Urban Guerrilla, White Collar Politics, The State in Modern Society,* and is coauthor of *A Manual for Direct Action,* which was used by civil rights workers in the mid-1960s. He has twice been awarded Fulbright fellowships to teach in Germany. Prior to coming to Rutgers, he was chairman of the sociology department at Lincoln University (Penn.), and taught at Haverford, Bryn Mawr, and Vassar. He and his family came to the United States in 1937 as refugees from Nazi Gemany.